John N Abbott

Summer Homes and Rambles Along the Erie Railway

A directory of reputable hotels, and boarding houses, in the most

charming of regions, within easy reach of New York; with distances, rates

of fare, terms of board, &c. Vol. 1

John N Abbott

Summer Homes and Rambles Along the Erie Railway
A directory of reputable hotels, and boarding houses, in the most charming of regions, within easy reach of New York; with distances, rates of fare, terms of board, &c. Vol. 1

ISBN/EAN: 9783337393489

Printed in Europe, USA, Canada, Australia, Japan

Cover: Foto ©Lupo / pixelio.de

More available books at **www.hansebooks.com**

SUMMER HOMES AND RAMBLES

ALONG THE

ERIE RAILWAY

A DIRECTORY

OF REPUTABLE HOTELS AND BOARDING HOUSES IN THE MOST
CHARMING OF REGIONS, WITHIN EASY REACH OF
NEW YORK; WITH DISTANCES, RATES OF
FARE, TERMS OF BOARD, &c., &c.

TOGETHER WITH

A DIGEST OF THE GAME AND FISH LAWS

GENERAL PASSENGER DEPARTMENT

1883

CONTENTS.

NEW YORK:
MARTIN B. BROWN, Printer and Stationer,
49 & 51 Park Place.
1883.

A Word With You.

To ALL who are seeking a summer home where perfect healthfulness is combined with all that attracts and pleases in natural surroundings, this little pamphlet is offered with the greatest confidence that they will find somewhere in its pages the mention of just such a place as they are desirous of securing. Nowhere within the same distance of New York is there a region so varied in physical characteristics; so well-calculated to afford a summering place suited to the widely different tastes and wants of the great army of city people who annually flock to the country, as the territory through which the Erie Railway passes for the first hundred miles or so of its route, and into which its branches enter in all directions. The quiet pleasures of farm life; the rugged beauty of mountain resorts; the retreats by hill-environed lakes, streams in picturesque valleys, and amid the rush and roar of cataracts; the wilds and haunts of the sportsman with his rod or gun—these are all at the command of the summer sojourner whose good fortune leads him to choose from the unrivaled "Erie territory." The farthest of these "homes of health" is but 160 miles from New York, a distance that is but short when overcome by the fast Erie trains that hurry the fugitive from city heat and turmoil to pleasant asylums in an enchanted summer land.

An important feature of the mountain retreats reached only by the Erie Railway is the absence of those pests and plagues, mosquitos and malaria. It has been also demonstrated conclusively that sufferers from pulmonary and bronchial affections are greatly benefited even by brief sojourns at these resorts, especially in the Ramapo Valley, among the Highlands of the Hudson, the mountains of Ulster, Sullivan and Pike counties, and along the Delaware Valley.

The purpose of this pamphlet is to give to those who are looking for

3

attractive localities in which to spend the summer all information that they will be likely to need in making such selection. The information is given in concise form, and every care has been taken to have it reliable and complete. It has been the intention of this Company to place in the book the names only of such boarding-house and hotel keepers as could be recommended to the most particular person, and every inquiry in the regions where they are located has been made to that end.

The Company requests, as a special favor, that any person who may select a boarding-place from this directory, and does not find it as it is represented, will notify the General Passenger Agent to that effect, in order that the house may not receive the indorsement of the publication another year.

A second edition of "Summer Home and Rambles," with additional names of boarding houses and hotels, will be published early in May.

ÁLONG THE ʿEASTERN ÐIVISION.

RUTHERFORD, BERGEN COUNTY, N. J.

9½ miles from New York.   15 trains each way daily ; 5 from and 3 to New York Sunday.

FARE—LOCAL, 30 CENTS ; EXCURSION, 40 CENTS.   COMMUTATION, 3 MONTHS, $19.00.

A place of suburban homes.   Pure water in abundance.   Fine fishing and boating in the Passaic river.   Woodcock and snipe.   Splendid drives, walks and shade.

BOARDING HOUSES.

"LYNDHURST"—*D. H. Speer, Manager, Lyndhurst P. O.*—1 mile. Accommodates 20 ; 14 rooms ; adults, $5 to $7 ; children, $2.50 to $4 ; servants, $5 ; $2 per day.   Discount for season.   Farm attached.   On Passaic river.   Boats and tackle, $1 per day.   Raise vegetables ; plenty of eggs, milk, poultry, etc.

Mrs. C. Van Riper—Five minutes from depot.   Accommodates 10 ; 7 rooms ; $6 ; $1 per day.   Raises vegetables.

PASSAIC, PASSAIC COUNTY, N. J.

12¼ miles from New York.   15 trains from and 17 to New York daily ; 6 from and 4 to New York Sunday.

FARE—LOCAL, 40 CENTS ; EXCURSION, 55 CENTS.   COMMUTATION, 3 MONTHS, $21.00.

Residence of many New York business men.   Churches of several denominations.   Best schools.   Dundee lake three miles distant—reached by charming drive.   In the heart of the Passaic Valley.   Fine boating and fishing in the Passaic river.   P. O. address for Passaic Bridge.

BOARDING HOUSE.

Mrs. John S. Conklin—½ mile from depot, at Passaic Bridge station. Free transportation.   Accommodates 13 ; 8 rooms ; adults, $6 to $8 ; children, $3 to $5 ; servants, $4 to $5.   Raises vegetables.   Plenty of shade. Large grounds.   Stream of running water.   Fruits.

KIP MANSION—*J. M. Seymour, Proprietor*—Near depot.   Accommodations for 30 ; 16 rooms ; $6 to $8 for one ; $12 to $22 for two ; $1.50 to $2 per day.   Open all the year.   Rooms large and airy.   Bathroom and closets.   Broad piazzas and well shaded grounds.

5

CLIFTON, PASSAIC COUNTY, N. J.

13½ miles from New York. 11 trains from and 15 to New York daily; 3 trains from and 3 to New York Sunday.

FARE—LOCAL, 45 CENTS; EXCURSION, 65 CENTS. COMMUTATION, 3 MONTHS, $21.

A charming rural spot. Fine drives to Paterson, Passaic, Rutherford, Hackensack and Belleville. Dundee lake, a popular resort for boating and fishing within a short walk. Healthful surroundings. Good water.

HOTEL.

CLIFTON GROVE HOUSE—*Robert Cunningham, Proprietor*—Near depot. Accommodations for 50; 30 rooms; $8 to $10. Rooms large and airy. Cottage near. Large picnic grove attached.

HAWTHORNE, PASSAIC COUNTY, N. J.

18½ miles from New York. 6 trains from and 7 trains to New York daily; 4 trains from and 3 to New York Sunday.

FARE—LOCAL, 60 CENTS; EXCURSION, 85 CENTS. COMMUTATION, 3 MONTHS, $23.50.

Preakness Hills on the west. Farming neighborhood. Elevated ground. Good fishing in the Passaic. Fine drives. Livery at Paterson. Passaic Falls, 1 mile.

BOARDING HOUSES.

C. J. Ackerman—½ mile from depot. Accommodations for 8; 7 rooms; adults, $6 to $7; servants, $5. Raises vegetables.

Mrs. James Fenner—½ mile from depot. Accommodations for 12; adults, $6 to $7; children and servants, half price; $1 per day. Specialty of fresh eggs, poultry and milk. Raises vegetables. P. O. address, Paterson, N. J.

RIDGEWOOD, BERGEN COUNTY, N. J.

22 miles from New York. 8 trains from and 7 to New York daily; 4 trains from and 3 to New York Sunday.

FARE—LOCAL, 70 CENTS; EXCURSION, 95 CENTS. COMMUTATION, 3 MONTHS, $25.

In Paramus Valley. Residence of celebrated public men. Much of antiquarian interest. Best of drives.

FARM HOUSE.

George J. Hopper—1¼ miles. Accommodations for 8 adults; 8 rooms; $7. Plenty of shade. Vegetables and fruit in abundance.

Mrs. E. D. Keeley, P. O. Box 34—½ mile. Accommodations for 30; $8 to $10 per week. Rooms large and airy. Broad piazza. Extensive views over the Hohokus and Ridgewood valley. High ground. Fine walks and drives. House and accommodations superior in every respect. Accommodations for horses and carriages.

HOHOKUS, BERGEN COUNTY, N. J.

23½ miles from New York. 7 trains from and 8 to New York daily ; 4 trains from and 3 to New York Sunday. -

FARE—LOCAL, 75 CENTS ; EXCURSION, $1. COMMUTATION, 3 MONTHS, $26.

Revolutionary ground. Residence of Joseph Jefferson, the celebrated actor. Ancient church, turned into a prison for American prisoners by the British, still standing. Fine drives and walks. Woodcock, quail, pickerel.

BOARDING HOUSES.

J. A. Osborne—½ mile from depot. Free transportation to and from two trains, morning and evening. Accommodations for 20 ; 9 rooms ; adults, $8 ; children and servants, $4 ; $1 50 per day. Discount for season. Vegetables and fruit from the farm. Eggs, milk, poultry. Old-fashioned farm-house.

John. Q. Voorhees—¾ mile. Free conveyance. Accommodations for 15 ; 3 single rooms ; 3 double ; $7 ; $1.50 per day. Raises vegetables.

SHADY BROOK FARM—*J. N. Leamon*—1½ mile. Free carriage ; Accommodations for 20 ; 10 rooms ; adults, $7 to $8 ; children and servants, half price; $1.50 per day. On Saddle river; boats free. 60 acres. Spring water. Plenty shade. Good drives. Vegetables, fruit, eggs, Alderney milk, butter, chickens.

VALLEY FARM—*John A. Zabriskie, Proprietor* —1 mile from depot. Free carriage. Accommodations for 20 ; 11 rooms ; adults, $7 to $8 ; $1.50 per day. Raises vegetables. Alderney milk, butter, chickens, etc., from farm.

BROOKSIDE FARM—*H. C. Dennett, Proprietor*—1 mile. Conveyance, regular trains free. Accommodate 30 ; 13 rooms ; adults, $8 to $10 ; children, half price ; no nurse-girls; $1.50 per day. From Saturday night till Monday morning, $3 50. Stream for boating on the premises. Boats free. Pure drinking water. Plenty of fresh vegetables, eggs, milk, and poultry.

WOODLAND HOUSE—*J. H. Bampber, Proprietor*—½ mile. Conveyance, 1 morning and 2 afternoon trains, free. Accommodate 25 ; 14 rooms ; $2 per day ; $3 from Saturday night until Monday morning. Near Saddle river, Sylvan lake, Franklin lake,· Ryerson lake. Furnish boats and tackle. Guides. Livery, $4 per day. Raise vegetables, plenty of milk, eggs and poultry.

W. A. Ackerman—Two miles from depot. Free transportation. Accommodation for 15 ; 11 rooms ; adults $7 ; children, $3.50 ; servants $3.50 ; $1 per day. Raises vegetables ; specialty of fresh milk, eggs and poultry. High ground. P. O. address, Saddle River, Bergen Co., N. J.

RAMSEY'S, BERGEN COUNTY, N. J.

27¾ miles from New York. 8 trains each way daily ; 5 trains from and 3 to New York Sunday.

FARE—LOCAL, 85 CENTS ; EXCURSION. $1.15. COMMUTATION, 3 MONTHS, $29.

Outlet of Ramapo Valley. Darlington, the famous stock farm of A. B. Darling, of the Fifth Avenue Hotel, is near. Healthful. Splendid drives. Great fruit-growing region. Fowler's livery ; $3 to $5 per day, according to rig.

BOARDING HOUSES.

A. De Baun—2½ miles. Post Office address, Saddle River, N. J. Conveyance free. Accommodate 30 ; 9 rooms ; adults, $8 to $9 ; children under 12, half price ; servants, $6 ; 50 cents per meal. On Saddle river. Raises vegetables and fruits. Meet guests at station. Stabling.

SHADY LAWN HOUSE—*A. H. Ackerman, Proprietor*—1 mile from depot. Conveyance free. Accommodate 25 ; 12 rooms. Horses and carriages furnished. Mountain scenery. Plenty of shade. Fresh vegetables, fruit, milk, butter and eggs on farm.

D. W. Valentine—Near depot. Accommodate 12. 5 rooms ; adults, $7 to $8 ; children and servants, $4. Raises vegetables ; milk and eggs in abundance.

Mrs. J. W. Valentine—Near depot. Accommodations for 15 ; 5 single rooms ; 5 double ; adults, $6 to $8 ; children, $3 to $4 ; servants, $5 ; $1.25 per day ; 50 cents per meal ; liberal discount to season guests. High ground. Fresh vegetables, milk, butter, eggs, poultry.

FARM HOUSES.

Isaac Ramsey—1 mile from depot. Accommodations for 25 ; 12 rooms ; adults, $8 to $10 ; children, $5 ; servants, $5. Raises vegetables.

A. H. Ackerman—1½ mile from depot. Accommodations for 15. Horses and carriages.

MAHWAH, BERGEN COUNTY, N. J.

30 miles from New York ; 7 trains from and 8 trains to New York daily ; 5 trains from and 4 to New York Sunday.

FARE—LOCAL, 95 CENTS ; EXCURSION, $1.25. COMMUTATION, 3 MONTHS, $30.

The beginning of the celebrated Ramapo Valley scenery. Mountain air, spring water, good drives, cool retreats.

SUMMER HOTEL.

MOUNTAIN VIEW HOUSE—*David Fox, Proprietor*—1 mile from depot. Same distance from Suffern. Free transportation in covered side-seat stage. Accommodations for 70 ; 35 rooms ; adults, $8 to $10 ; children, $5 to $8 ;

servants, $5 ; $2.50 per day. Can furnish boats, fishing-tackle and guns, at reasonable charge. Proprietor or his man acts as guide at reasonable rates. Furnishes livery to sportsmen ; $5 per day for team and man. General livery charge, $1.00, $1.50 per hour. Furnishes a four-in-hand for pleasure driving, at a reasonable charge. Saddle horses for ladies and gentlemen. Fine croquet ground, billiard table, etc. Best of references from former guests. Raises vegetables, fruits, etc. P. O. address, Suffern, N. Y., or Mahwah, N. J.

BOARDING HOUSE.

Mrs. D. W. Hopper—1 mile from depot. Accommodation for 15 ; 3 single rooms ; 3 double rooms ; $8 single ; $16 double ; children half price ; $2 per day. No discount. Raises vegetables.

SUFFERN, ROCKLAND COUNTY, N. Y.

32 miles from New York ; 9 trains from and 11 to New York ; 6 trains from and 5 to New York Sunday.

FARE—LOCAL, $1 ; EXCURSION, $1.35. COMMUTATION, 3 MONTHS, $31.

At the base of the southern Highlands of the Hudson, in the rocky pass of the Ramapo. Once Washington's headquarters. Famous ground in the Revolution. High hills on every side. Magnificent views. A resort for sufferers with bronchial and pulmonary affections. Recommended by leading physicians. Many natural curiosities. Boarding houses all first-class. Bass and pickerel fishing. Partridge, quail and woodcock. Negro lake, 4 miles ; Shippen lake, 6 miles ; Sterling lake, 12 miles.

BOARDING HOUSES.

T. W. Suffern—2/3 of a mile ; 500 feet above sea level. Transportation free. Accommodations for 30 ; 17 rooms ; adults, $10. Raises vegetables. Boats and fishing-tackle free. Acts as guide to lakes free to guests. Free carriage.

C. A. Wannemaker—Near depot. Accommodations for 10 ; 6 rooms ; prices moderate. Raises vegetables.

R. S. De Witt—¾ of a mile. Conveyances free. Accommodations for 8 ; 4 rooms ; adults, $8 to $12 ; children and servants half price. In a valley foot of densely wooded mountain. All modern improvements. Modern furniture. 25 acres in fruit ; strawberries, blackberries, raspberries, a specialty. 3 acres vegetable garden. Ice house. Fine well water. Everything fresh, and in great abundance.

FARM HOUSES.

Augustus Coe—2½ miles from depot. Transportation free. Accommodations for 15 ; adults, $6 to $8 ; children under 12, half price ; servants, $5. Farm produce, eggs, milk, poultry. Excellent stabling.

Lawrence D. N. Coe.—2 miles. Accommodations for 30 ; 16 rooms ; adults, $ 6 to $8 ; children, half price ; 50 cents per meal. Discount to season guests. Furnishes livery. Raises own vegetables on farm. Eggs and milk a specialty.

SLOATSBURG, ROCKLAND COUNTY, N. Y.

35½ miles from New York. 4 trains from and 3 to New York daily ; 4 from and 2 to New York Sunday.

FARE—LOCAL, $1.10 ; EXCURSION, $1.45. COMMUTATION, 3 MONTHS, $35.50.

Center of sporting region. Lorillard's Lake, 3 miles ; Potague Lake, 1 mile ; Cedar Lake, 2 miles ; others in the vicinity. Romantic drives. Bass and pickerel fishing. Good hunting. Lakes from 500 to 1,000 feet above tide. Wild surroundings. Partridge, woodcock and quail.

HOTEL.

"ROCKLAND HOTEL "—*Post & Hughes, Proprietors*—Near depot ; ½ mile from Sterling Junction. Accommodations for 25 ; 15 rooms ; adults, $8 ; children and servants, $5 ; $2 per day ; discount for season. Livery attached. Guides, $2 per day. Plenty fresh milk, eggs and poultry.

LORILLARD'S, ROCKLAND COUNTY, N. Y.

38½ miles from New York. 2 trains to and 1 from New York daily ; 1 each way Sunday.

FARE—LOCAL, $1.20 ; EXCURSION, $1.60.

STATION FOR LORILLARD'S OR TRUXEDO LAKE.—*Property of Lorillard estate.*—1 mile from station. 500 feet above tide. Black bass, pickerel and perch. Privilege of fishing, $5 per rod per day, boat included. Conveyance furnished from station to lake on notice to Josiah Patterson, Sloatsburg, Rockland County, N. Y., 50 cents each way. Guide, $2 per day.

SOUTHFIELDS, ORANGE COUNTY, N. Y.

42 miles from New York. 4 trains each way daily ; 4 trains from and 2 to New York on Sunday.

FARE—LOCAL, $1 30 ; EXCURSION, $1.75. COMMUTATION, 3 MONTHS, $39.

Station from which the lakes are readily reached ; Truxedo, 3 miles ; Mambasha, 3 miles. Good roads. Livery in the place. Partridge, quail, rabbits, duck and woodcock.

BOARDING HOUSE.

C. A. Walworth—Short walk from depot. Accommodate 36 ; 16 rooms ; adults, $8 to $10 ; children, $4 ; servants, $5 ; $2 per day. Base of mountains. Lake on mountain, back of house. Raises vegetables. Boat and tackle, $1 per day. Guides, $2 per day. Dogs and equipments, no extra charge.

10

TURNER'S, ORANGE COUNTY, N. Y.

47½ miles from New York.   10 trains from New York daily and 6 on Sunday ; 8 trains to
New York daily and 6 on Sunday.

FARE—LOCAL, $1.45 ; EXCURSION, $1.95.   COMMUTATION, 3 MONTHS, $42.

(Change cars for Central Valley, Highland Mills, Woodbury, Mountainville, Cornwall
and Newburgh.)

Last resort in Ramapo Valley. Famous as dining station on the Erie
Railway. Beginning of celebrated Orange County dairy region. Near all
the lakes mentioned. Partridge, quail, woodcock.   Slaughter lake, 3
miles ; Rumsey lake, 2 miles ; Little Long, 3½ miles ; Mambasha, 4 miles ;
Round lake, 3 miles.   Bass, pickerel, perch. Livery in place. Guides,
$2 per day.

BOARDING HOUSES.

Mrs. R. McKelvey—¾ of mile. $1 for family and baggage. Accommo-
date 20 ; 7 rooms ; adults, $6 to $8 : children, $3 to $5 ; servants, $4 to $5 ;
$1.25 per day. Discount for season. All the lakes easy of access. Vege-
tables, fruits, eggs, milk and butter.

N. B. Starkweather—½ mile. Accommodate 30 ; adults, $7 to $10 ;
children, half price, or by agreement ; servants, half price ; $1.50 per day.
Horses and wagons for use of guests. Farm of 30 acres. Fresh milk,
cream, eggs and poultry.

Gilbert Turner—Accommodations for 20 ; $6 to $9.

Mrs. W. C. Smith—1 mile. Transportation free. Accommodations for
30 ; 10 rooms ; adults, $8 to $10 ; children under 12, $5 ; servants, $6 ;
$1.50 per day. Farm house. Fresh farm produce of all kinds. P. O. Box
53.

Mrs. P. Turner—(Hotel)—Accommodations for 20 ; $6 to $10.

Mrs. J. R. Tapping—Short walk. Accommodate 12 ; 6 rooms ; adults,
$6 to $7 ; children, half price ; 35 cents meal ; discount for season. Raises
vegetables.

MONROE, ORANGE COUNTY, N. Y.

49¾ miles from New York. 6 trains from and 7 to New York daily ; 4 trains each
way Sunday.

FARE—LOCAL, $1.55 ; EXCURSION, $2.05. COMMUTATION, 3 MONTHS, $44.

Among the dairy farms. Highest elevation of any station on the Erie,
east of Shawangunk mountains. Lakes and streams, and mountains. Highlands, 2 miles westward. Greenwood Lake, 9 miles. Splendid drives.
Monroe, Round, Mambasha, Walton, and Long ponds near. Black bass,
pickerel, perch, woodcock, quail, rabbits. Fishing tackle furnished at lakes.
Good livery in place.

HOTELS.

SEVEN SPRINGS MOUNTAIN HOUSE—*C. E. Davidson, Proprietor*—Two
miles from depot. Stages and carriages. Accommodations for 400 ; up-
wards of 200 rooms ; adults, $9 to $18 ; children under 7 half rate ; servants

11

half rate ; $3.00 per day. Discount to season guests. 2,000 feet above tide, summit of Schunemunk mountain. Fine mountain retreat. Hotel entirely refitted, repainted, etc. Three spacious stone buildings, connected by covered walks. Band of music. Ball room 60 feet square. Saddle horses and riding masters. Extended view of most picturesque portion of Orange County. Pure dry air, beneficial in pulmonary complaints. Mineral spring for rheumatism, kidney and liver diseases. Billiards, croquet, archery. Dancing every night. Livery attached. Hotel filled last season. Table furnished with the best only. Stages connect with every train. Best city references.

J. J. Van Duzer—Near depot. Accommodations for 20 ; 10 rooms ; five single and connecting for families ; adults $6 to $10 ; $2 per day. Discount for season. Raises vegetables. Plenty of eggs, milk, poultry, etc.

BOARDING HOUSES.

W. R. Conkling—¾ mile. Free conveyance. Accommodations for 15 ; adults, $6 and $7 ; children, half price ; servants, $4 and $5 ; $1.50 from Saturday till Monday morning. Raises vegetables. Fresh milk, poultry and eggs. Parties invited to come and inspect place.

P. C. Hager—¼ mile. Accommodations for 12 ; 8 rooms ; adults, $6 to $8 ; children under 12, half price ; servants, $5 ; $1.50 per day. Furnishes livery. Long pond, 1 mile. Raises vegetables. Plenty of fresh eggs, milk and poultry.

GRANITE HOUSE—Short walk. Accommodations for 40 ; 18 rooms ; adults, $8 to $10 ; children under 12, $5 ; servants, $5 ; $1.50 per day. Beautiful lawn. Fine shade. Farm 15 acres. Vegetables, milk, cream, eggs, butter, fruit, all from the farm. References given and required.

Mrs. H. S. Carpenter—½ mile. Accommodations for 15 ; 6 rooms ; adults, $10 ; children under 10, $4 ; servants, $5 ; 40 cents a meal. Raises vegetables. Plenty fresh milk, eggs and poultry.

Mrs. P. A. McNally—½ mile. Accommodations for 20 ; adults, $8 to $10 ; $2 per day. Raises vegetables. Plenty fresh milk, eggs, poultry, etc.

Thomas Caren—1 mile. Transportation, 25 cents. Accommodations for 30 ; 15 rooms ; adults, $7 to $8 ; children and servants, $4 ; $1.35 per day. Discount for season. Shade, hammocks, swings, croquet lawns, piano. High ground. Raises vegetables. Guides on place. Furnishes livery.

James Cregen—2 miles. Covered stage, free. Accommodations for 25 ; 15 rooms ; adults, $7 ; children and servants, half price. Discount for season. Plenty eggs, milk, butter, fresh vegetables.

FARM HOUSES.

Uriah Crosson—2½ miles from depot. Transportation, Saturday evening and Monday morning, free ; at other times, 50 cents. Accommodations for 10 ; 7 rooms ; adults, $7 ; children, half rate ; servants, $5 ; $1 per day. No discount. Raise vegetables.

Wm. Sutherland—¼ mile from depot. Accommodations for 12 ; $6 ; $1.50 per day.

Mrs. J. Nelson Bull—2½ miles. Conveyance free. Accommodations for 10 ; 8 rooms ; adults, $8 ; children and servants, $4 ; $1.50 per day. Plenty of fresh eggs, milk, poultry, etc.

Charles Hunter—¼ mile. Accommodations for 12 ; 6 rooms ; adults, $6 to $8 ; children, $3 to $4 ; servants, $5. Vegetables, eggs, milk and butter from farm.

OXFORD, ORANGE COUNTY, N. Y.

52¼ miles from New York. 4 trains each way daily ; 4 trains from and 3 to New York on Sunday.

FARE—LOCAL, $1.60 ; EXCURSION, $2.15. COMMUTATION, 3 MONTHS, $45.50.

Fine scenery, lakes and streams, pure air and water have made this a popular retreat. Greenwood lake, 9 miles. P. O. address, Oxford depot, Orange Co., N. Y.

FARM BOARDING HOUSES.

A. H. Laurence—1 mile. Free transportation. Accommodations for 10 ; 8 rooms ; adults, $7 ; children under 10, half price ; servants, $5 ; $1 per day. High ground. View of the Catskills. Meet guests on notice.

Joseph W. Youngs—Near depot. Accommodate 20 ; 10 rooms ; adults, $8 ; children, $4 ; servants, $5 ; $1.50 per day. Furnish teams and guides ; guides, $2 per day ; teams, $1 an hour. Farm house. Raises vegetables. Poultry, eggs and milk always fresh.

A. Y. Clark—Accommodations for 30 ; $5 to $8.

GREYCOURT, ORANGE COUNTY, N. Y.

54¼ miles from New York. 6 trains from and 7 to New York daily ; 4 trains each way Sunday.

FARE—LOCAL, $1.65 ; EXCURSION, $2.25. COMMUTATION, 3 MONTHS, $46.50.

(Change cars for Warwick (see page 38), Craigville, Washingtonville, Salisbury and Newburgh (see page 38.

Junction of the Newburg Branch and Lehigh and Hudson River Railroad with the main line of the Erie. Former follows valley of Murderer's Kill. Other around base of the Sugar-Loaf mountain.

HOTEL.

GREYCOURT HOUSE—*John R. Procter, Proprietor*—Near depot. Accommodations for 10 ; 12 rooms ; adults, $10 ; children, $5 ; servants, $7; $2 per day. Raises vegetables. Livery. P. O. address, Chester, N. Y.

FARM HOUSE.

J. M. Seeley—One mile from depot. Free transportation. Accommodations for 20 ; $4 to $8. Farm House large and commodious. Raises vegetables. Plenty of fresh milk, eggs and poultry. P. O. address, Oxford Depot, Orange County, N. Y.

CHESTER, ORANGE COUNTY. N. Y.

55¼ miles from New York. 6 trains from and 7 to New York daily. 4 trains each way Sunday.

FARE—LOCAL, $1.70 ; EXCURSION, $2.30. COMMUTATION, 3 MONTHS, $47.25.

Aquiet, agricultural neighborhood. Good drives. Fine scenery. Quail and woodcock. Black bass and pickerel near. Glenmere lake. Livery, $2.50 to $3 per day.

OLD-FASHIONED FARM HOUSE.

George Seely—1¼ mile. Accommodations for 8 ; 4 rooms ; adults, $6 to $8 ; children, 4 ; servants, $3 to $4 ; $1.50 per day. Discount for season. Streams close by the house. Elevated location; maple shade. Vegetables and fruits from farm. Stabling.

GOSHEN, ORANGE COUNTY, N. Y.

59¾ miles from New York. 10 trains from and 11 to New York daily ; 5 trains from and 6 to New York Sunday.

FARE—LOCAL, $1.85; EXCURSION, $2.50. COMMUTATION, 3 MONTHS, $50.

(Change cars for Montgomery, Lake Mohunk and Lake Minnewaska (New Paaltz, see page 23), and all resorts under head of "In the Catskills" (see page 39).

Famous for its butter, milk and blooded horses. The stock farms in and near Goshen are celebrated all over the Union. An interesting locality for summer sojourners and tourists. Black bass fishing in the Wallkill river and Pochunk creek. Several lakes easy of access. Drives excellent. Good livery.

BOARDING HOUSE.

William Goldthwaite—¼ mile. Accommodations for 12 ; 12 rooms ; adults, $5 to $7 ; children, half price ; servants, $4 ; 10 per cent. discount for season. Especially favorable for children ; Facing large park. Large schoolroom for playroom. School boarding house.

FARM HOUSES.

GOLDEN HILL FARM—*J. A. Brewster*—1½ miles. Accommodate 5 ; 5 rooms ; adults, $10 ; servants, $8.

Daniel D. Banker—2½ miles. Convey season boarders free. Accommodate 30 ; 13 rooms ; adults, $7 to $10 ; children under 12, $4 ; servants, $5. Good stabling. Orange dairy farm. Best of references.

14

S. S. Gregory—1½ miles. Free transportation. Accommodations for 16 adults ; 8 rooms ; $6 to $8 ; servants, $5 ; $1.50 per day ; discount for season. Guides. Livery. Farm produce of all kinds.

MONTGOMERY, ORANGE COUNTY, N. Y.

10 miles from Goshen on Montgomery branch. 2 trains each way daily ; 2 trains each way Sunday.

FARE—LOCAL, $2.20 ; EXCURSION, $3. COMMUTATION, 3 MONTHS, $50.

HOTEL.

PALACE HOTEL—*E. J. Emerson, Proprietor*—Short walk. Accommodate 40 ; adults, $7 to $10 ; children and servants, $5 to $7 ; $2 per day ; discount for season. Good fishing and boating in Wallkill river. Good drives. New hotel. Romantic portion of Wallkill Valley. Raises vegetables. Specialty of fresh milk, eggs and poultry. Livery attached ; $3 and $5 per day.

FARM HOUSE.

Marcus Rumpf—3½ miles. Free conveyance. Accommodate 25 ; 7 rooms ; 4 of them family rooms, accommodating 4 in each ; adults, $6 to $7 ; children under 10, $3 ; under 14 years, $4 ; servants, $4 to $5 ; $1 per day. Farm. Plenty fresh eggs, milk, butter and vegetables.

MIDDLETOWN, ORANGE COUNTY, N. Y.

67 miles from New York. 7 trains from and 9 to New York daily ; 4 trains from and 6 to New York on Sunday.

FARE—LOCAL, $2.05 ; EXCURSION, $2.75. COMMUTATION, 3 MONTHS, $53.

(Change cars at Main street for Ellenville, Fallsburg, and Stations on the Midland Railroad (see page 22).

Clean, broad streets, pure water, perfect drainage. Fine residences, grounds, drives, hills, woods and valleys. Orange County dairy region. Pickerel and bass fishing in the Wallkill. Trout streams of Sullivan County easy of access. Woodcock and quail shooting. While there are no hotels or boarding houses in Middletown which make a specialty of keeping summer boarders, it is the station from which several of the most charming localities in the great Orange County dairy region are reached. These are along the Erie's

CRAWFORD BRANCH,

which extends from Middletown to Pine Bush, a distance of 13 miles. At the villages located on the Branch the summer boarder will find typical farm homes, where health, wealth and plenty abound. This Crawford region is not surpassed anywhere in quiet, pastoral beauty. The country is high and varied. The Wallkill river is near, and the hills, streams and lakes of Sullivan County within easy reach.

CIRCLEVILLE, ORANGE COUNTY, N. Y.

5 miles from Middletown. 2 trains from and to New York daily ; 1 on Sundays.

FARE—LOCAL, $2.20 ; EXCURSION, $3. COMMUTATION, 3 MONTHS, $57.50.

BOARDING HOUSES.

A. B. Jordan—Near. Accommodation for 20 ; 11 rooms ; adults, $5 to $10 ; children under 10, half price ; servants, $5 ; $1 per day. Discount for season. Raises vegetables. Abundance of fresh butter, eggs, milk and poultry. Livery in the place.

H. S. Wilkison—¾ mile. Conveyance free. Accommodations for 20 ; 9 rooms ; adults, $5 to $6 ; children under 12, $3 ; servants, $3 and $4 ; $1 per day. Discount for season. Large house. High ground. Rooms high and airy. Pure water ; ice. No fogs. Organ, croquet, swing. Grove near house. Hammocks, etc. Fine view of Shawangunk mountains. Excellent place for families. Everything fresh daily from farm.

William H. Bull—½ mile from depot. Accommodations for 10 ; 15 rooms ; rates on application. Hunting equipments free. Raise vegetables. Plenty of milk, eggs and poultry.

Charles Kelso—½ mile from depot. Accommodations for 6 ; 5 rooms ; rates on application. Specialty of eggs, milk and poultry. Raise vegetables. Plenty of fruit.

PINE BUSH.

13 miles from Middletown. 2 trains from and to New York daily ; 1 on Sunday.

FARE—LOCAL, $2.45 ; EXCURSION, $3.30. COMMUTATION, 3 MONTHS, $61.

BOARDING HOUSES.

R. L. Thompson—3 miles. Conveyance, season guests and baggage free ; Accommodation for 16 ; 6 rooms ; adults, $8 ; children under 10 years half price ; no servants ; transient, $1.25 per day. Discount for season. Raise vegetables. Plenty of milk, eggs, and poultry.

C. J. Falconer—Near depot. Accommodation for 14 ; 6 rooms ; adults, $5 to $6 ; children under 10 years half price ; servants, $4 ; $1 per day. Discount for season. Raises vegetables. Plenty of milk, eggs, and poultry.

Mary E. Dey—Near depot. Accommodation for 12 ; 6 rooms ; adults, $5 to $6 ; children under 10 years and servants, half price ; $1 per day. Discount for season. Fine mountain view. Plenty of shade. Raise vegetables. Plenty of milk, eggs, and poultry.

16

OTISVILLE, ORANGE COUNTY, N. Y.

— ——

75¼ miles from New York. 3 trains from and 4 to New York daily ; 2 from and 3 to New York Sunday.

FARE—LOCAL, $2.35 ; EXCURSION, $3.10. COMMUTATION, 3 MONTHS, $58.50.

A quiet farming neighborhood, in the midst of the dairies. 1,200 feet above tide, on Shawangunk range. Woodcock shooting in season. Livery, $3 to $7 per day.

FARM BOARDING HOUSE.

James B. Wiggins—2 miles. Free conveyance. Good road. 12 large, airy rooms. Accommodations for 25 ; adults, $5 to $6 (adults with few or no children preferred) ; children, according to size ; servants, $4 ; $1 per day. Discount for season. Guests wanted from 1st of June till late in Fall. House large. Broad lawn. Maple trees. Cottage, 9 rooms, near. Everything fresh from farm.

PRIVATE HOUSES.

Mrs. J. H. Reed—Short walk from depot. Accommodations for 12 ; 4 single rooms ; 4 double rooms ; $6 ; $1 per day. Raises vegetables.

Mrs. M. E. Wilkin—Near. 5 rooms. Adults, $6 ; children under 10, $4; servants, $4; $1 per day. Discount for families. Half mile from summit of Shawangunk mountains. Fresh milk, eggs, etc. Raises vegetables.

Mrs. Asa J. Ogden—Near depot. Accommodate 8 ; 4 large rooms ; adults, $6 ; children and servants, $4. Raises vegetables. Large yard. Fruit. Quiet location. Plenty eggs, milk, poultry, etc.

Mrs. M. J. Green—Near. Accommodate 20 ; 10 rooms ; adults, $6 ; children, under 10, $4 ; servants, $4 ; $1 per day. Discount for families. Rooms large and airy. Fresh milk, eggs and butter and vegetables from the place.

Mrs. L. Drake —½ mile. Conveyance free. Accommodations for 10 ; 5 rooms ; adults, $6 ; children, under 12, $3 ; servants, $4 ; $1 per day. Raises vegetables. Plenty of fresh eggs, milk and poultry.

S. A. Ketcham—Near. Accommodations for 12 ; 8 rooms ; adults, $5 to $7 ; children, as to age ; servants, $4 to $5 ; $1 per day. Discount for season. Retired spot, on outskirts of village. Plenty of shade. Horses and carriages. Fresh vegetables, milk, eggs and poultry.

FARM HOUSES.

S. Bertholf—1 mile. Free conveyance. Accommodate 15 ; adults, $5 to $6 ; $1 per day. Old-fashioned farm. Fine locality. Eggs, milk, butter and vegetables fresh daily.

W. C. Tymeson—¾ mile from depot. Free conveyance. Accommodate 30 ; 12 rooms ; adults, $6 ; children, $3 ; servants, $4 ; $1 per day. Large grounds. Lake on the premises. Free boats. Raises vegetables. Plenty of fresh eggs, milk and poultry.

17

H. W. Bull—¾ mile. Free conveyance. Accommodations for 15 ; adults, $6 ; children, $3 ; servants, $4 ; $1 per day. Vegetables raised on place. Specialty of eggs, milk and poultry.

PORT JERVIS, ORANGE COUNTY, N. Y.

88¼ miles from New York. 7 trains from and 8 to New York daily ; 4 from and 6 to New York Sunday.

FARE—LOCAL, $2.70 ; EXCURSION, $3.60. COMMUTATION, 3 MONTHS, $65.

(Change cars for Monticello and White Lake (see page 21) ; stages for Milford and Ding-man's Ferry (see page 18.)

Terminus of the Eastern and Delaware Divisions of the Erie Railway. Junction of the Port Jervis and Monticello Railroad. Station for Milford, Pa., Dingman's Ferry, Pa., and all the Lower Delaware valley resorts, and the famous trout streams, bass and pickerel lakes, and hunting grounds of Pike and Sullivan counties. Best of bass-fishing in the Delaware, at the village. Roomy coaches run between Port Jervis, Milford and Dingman's, the fare on which is 50 cents in the day time, and 75 cents at night. Private conveyance may be or-dered by telegraph of, J. Schorr, J. Findlay, Geo. Horton, Milford, Pa., Quick and Hulsizer, B. Godley, E. Slauson, T. Maguire, Port Jervis ; terms to Milford, single, $2 ; team, $4. To Dingmans, single, $3 ; team, $6.

FOWLER HOUSE—*R. C. Campbell, Proprietor*—1 block. Free 'bus to and from all trains. Accommodations for 50 ; 60 rooms ; $2 per day. Hotel newly appointed. Pleasant location. Every modern convenience. Hotel livery, B. Godley, Proprietor.

IN THE LOWER DELAWARE VALLEY.

MILFORD, PIKE COUNTY, PA.

A splendid drive of 7 miles from Port Jervis, down the Delaware Valley.

County-seat of the famous Pike County. Situated on a high bluff over-looking the Delaware river. Streets broad, free from dust, shaded, and hard as cement. The remarkable waterfalls on the Sawkill, Raymondskill, Sanvantine and Vandermark creeks, are from one to three miles from village. Milford Glen on the Sawkill, is a cool retreat in the village. Sawkill pond, Little Log Tavern pond, Big and Little Walker ponds, and Brink pond, are from 4 to 10 miles distant. Best of black bass and trout-fishing almost within the bounds of the village. Hotels and boarding-houses are all first-class. Presbyterian, Methodist, Episcopal, and Catholic churches. The drives are not surpassed by any city boulevard. The river road, from Port Jervis to Bushkill, 30 miles, is as smooth as a floor. Livery accommodations are excellent. No mosquitoes. No malaria. Guides procured by all the hotels and boarding-places.

HOTELS.

FAUCHERE HOUSE—*L. Fauchere, Proprietor*—Accommodate 200 ; 100 rooms ; adults, $14 to $18, according to room ; children and servants as agreed ; $2.50 per day. Discount for season. Central location. French style. Modern cottages attached. Vegetables raised on the premises and in the vicinity.

CRISSMAN HOUSE—*Frank Crissman, Proprietor*—Accommodate 100 ; 60 rooms ; adults, $8 to $10 ; $2 per day. Discount to season guests. Billiard parlor. Commodious stables. Fresh vegetables, milk, butter, and eggs from farm. Livery attached. Cottages near house. Sportsmen equipped.

SAWKILL HOUSE—*The Misses Cornelius, Proprietors*—Accommodate 75 ; 30 rooms ; adults, $8 to $10 ; children under 12 and servants, half price ; $2 per day. Discount for season. Patronized by leading families of New York, Brooklyn, and Philadelphia. Pleasant cottage near. No bar. Specialty, fresh milk, eggs, poultry, and vegetables.

RIVER VIEW HOUSE—*F. LeClerc, Proprietor*—Accommodate 45 ; 17 rooms ; adults, $12 ; children and servants half price ; $2 per day. Discount for season. Overlooks Delaware river. Large grounds. French style.

Gustave De Behrl's—Accommodate 75 ; 25 double, 12 single rooms ; $10 to $12 single, $20 to $25 double ; $2.50 per day. French cooking. Large garden. Fresh milk, eggs, and poultry from farm. Cottages attached.

J. K. Thornton—Accommodate 65 ; 45 rooms ; adults, $7 to $9 ; children, $4 to $5 ; servants, $4 ; $1.50 per day ; discount for season. Livery attached. Boat and tackle, $2 per day. Dogs and equipments, $1 per day. Vegetables from farm fresh every day.

BOARDING HOUSES.

BLUFF HOUSE—*Sawyer & Wells, Proprietors*—Accommodation for 100 ; 60 rooms ; adults, $9 to $18 ; children, $5 to $7 ; servants, $6 to $8 ; $2.50 to $3 per day. Discount for season. On banks of Delaware, 150 feet above. Extended view of valley. Broad verandas and balconies. Spring water throughout. Bath rooms. Four acres of grounds fronting on river. Raise most of vegetables used in house.

BARNES COTTAGE—*Mrs. H. Barnes, Proprietor*—Accommodate 50 ; 10 single rooms ; 10 double rooms ; adults, $7 ; children under 10, half price ; servants, half price ; $1.50 per day. Discount for season, $1 per week. One of the most pleasant locations in town. Milford Glen in the rear. Rooms cool and airy. Vegetables and fruits from the grounds and vicinity.

GLEN COTTAGE—*E. T. Reviere, Proprietor*—Accommodate 30 ; 18 rooms ; adults, $12 to $14 ; children, $10 to $12 ; servants, $9 to $10 ; $2 per day. Discount for season. Near famous Milford Glen. French style.

ARMSTRONG COTTAGE—*A. A. Armstrong, Proprietor*—Accommodate 20 at table ; 10 rooms ; adults from $8 to $12 ; children and servants, half price ; $1.50 per day. Discount for season. Pleasant location. Suitable cottages near. Fresh eggs, milk and poultry in abundance.

FARM BOARDING HOUSE.

CONASHAUGH FARM HOUSE.—*K. K. Van Etten, Proprietor*—4 miles from Milford. Stage from Port Jervis, $1 ; private conveyance, from $3 to $6 ; accommodations for 20 ; 8 rooms ; adults, $7 ; children under 5, half price. Discount for season. High ground. Near Delaware river. On bank of Conashaugh creek. Boating and fishing. Mountain scenery. Raises vegetables. Milk, eggs and vegetables.

DINGMAN'S FERRY, PIKE COUNTY, PA.

15 miles from Port Jervis. Stage connection. Fare, $1.

A resort in a part of the Delaware Valley, the character of whose surroundings has given it the name of the Switzerland of America. It is a region of cataracts, mountains, glens, gorges and wonderful lakes. Dingman's creek, Adam's brook, and Decker's creek, are successions of precipitous waterfalls for miles. Eight of these are within two miles of the village. The mountain drives are equal to those of the Catskills. The streams are famous for their trout. Silver lake and Lake Nichecronk, and Delaware river, afford the best of bass and pickerel fishing. No mosquitoes ; no malaria. Beneficial in hay-fever. Guides at fair rates.

HOTELS.

HIGH FALLS HOUSE —*Philip F. Fulmer, M. D., Proprietor*—Accommodate 200 ; 130 rooms ; adults, $10 ; children and servants, $5 ; $2 per day. Discount for season. Spring water. Table supplied from hotel garden. Rooms spacious and airy. Resort of men and women eminent in art, literature and science.

Ran. Van Gorden's—Accommodate 15 ; 12 rooms ; adults, $7 ; $1.50 per day. Fresh vegetables, milk, butter and eggs, from the farm daily. Table celebrated.

MANOR HOUSE —*John S. Van Campen, Proprietor*—½ mile from Dingman's village. Accommodation for 30 ; 14 rooms ; adults, $7 to $9 ; children, $3 to $5 ; servants, $4 ; $1.75 per day. On banks of Delaware. 3 miles of splendid boating. Boats furnished. Steamboat in the river for use of guests.

Among the Sullivan and Ulster Mountains.

◆

OAKLAND VALLEY, SULLIVAN COUNTY, N. Y.

13 miles from Port Jervis, on Port Jervis and Monticello Railroad.

A romantic village, surrounded by wild and picturesque scenery, Good trout fishing.

PRIVATE RESIDENCE.

Mrs. O. B. Wheeler, Jr.—Post Office address, Oakland Valley, Sullivan County, N. Y.—Short walk. Accommodations for 20 : 10 rooms ; adults, $8 : children and servants, $5 ; 11 and $1.50 per day. Best city references. Plenty of shade. Raises vegetables. Plenty eggs, milk, poultry, etc.

FARM BOARDING HOUSE.

James Ketcham—Near Oakland Station. P. O. address, Oakland Valley, Sullivan County, N. Y. Accommodate 40 ; 30 rooms : adults, $6 to $7 ; children under 12, half price ; $1 to $1.50 per day. Telegraph near. Best trout fishing and hunting. Pure spring water. House built expressly for city boarders. Raise all vegetables, and furnish fresh eggs, milk and poultry. Furnish livery. Obtain guides. Grove of forest trees. Numerous mountain springs.

A. S. Rhodes—½ mile from Paradise Station. P. O. address, Oakland Valley. A resort for sportsmen. Accommodations for gentlemen with horses, dogs, etc. Acts as guide to all streams, lakes and hunting grounds. Table well supplied.

MONTICELLO, SULLIVAN COUNTY, N. Y.

5 hours ride from New York, via Erie Railway to Port Jervis, thence by Port Jervis and Monticello Railroad. Close connections from Erie Depot.
FARE—LOCAL, $3.45. EXCURSION, $5.

Elevation 1,700 feet above tide. Surrounded by lakes, trout streams, and game preserves. Mountains, waterfalls. Pleasant lake, 1 mile ; Sackett, 4 miles ; White lake, 8 miles ; Black lake, 9 miles ; best bass, pickerel, and perch fishing. Trout streams near by. Guides, $1 per day. Deer, bear, foxes, partridge, quail, woodcock, English snipe, duck, wild pigeons in sea-

21

son. No malaria or fever. No mosquitoes. Paved walks. A beautiful public park. Hotels and boarding houses first-class in all respects. Mansion House unsurpassed.

HOTEL.

MANSION HOUSE.--*Le Grand Morris, Proprietor*—¼ mile. Free omnibus. Accommodate 100 ; 75 rooms ; adults, $8 to $10 ; children and servants, $5 ; $2 per day. Discount for season. Everything modern. Location central and pleasant. Rooms large. nicely furnished, ceilings high. Particular attention to table service. Best city references. Equips sportsmen free of charge. Boats free to guests. Fresh farm products. House highly recommended. Guides obtained.

BOARDING HOUSES.

TOWNER'S VILLA--*Mrs. R. B. Towner, Proprietress*—¾ mile. Accommodates 40; 18 rooms ; adults, $8 to $10 ; children and servants, half price; $1.50 per day. Discount for season. Finely situated. Grove in rear of grounds. Raises vegetables. Omnibus to and from every train, 15 cents. Milk, eggs and poultry always on hand.

SUNNY SIDE—*N. L. Stern*—¼ mile. Coach, 10 cents. Accommodate 15 ; 8 rooms ; adults, $10 ; children at first table, full price ; servants, half price ; $2 per day. Discount for season. Raises vegetables.

Mrs. Charles Burnham—¼ mile from depot. Accommodations for 15 ; adults, $8. Farm of 100 acres. Plenty shade. Raises vegetables. Abundance of fresh milk, eggs and poultry.

Charles Foster—P. O. address, Bethel, Sullivan County, N. Y. 10 miles either from Cochecton or Monticello. Daily mail stages. Accommodates 10 ; adults, $6. In vicinity of Beach lake, White lake, Lake Superior and Chestnut lake. Milk, eggs, poultry and vegetables fresh daily.

C. G. Royce—Near depot. Accommodate 40 ; 25 rooms ; adults, $5 to $7 ; children, $2 to $5 ; servants, $4 ; $1 per day. Discount for season. Plenty shade. Farm of 30 acres. Milk, eggs, butter poultry. Livery attached.

Mrs. M. B. Stewart—½ mile. Omnibus, 10 cents. Accommodate 25 ; 12 rooms ; adults, $8 to $10 ; prefer no children ; no deduction if taken. House new. Raise and buy vegetables. Fresh milk, eggs and poultry.

A. M. Fulton—¼ mile. Accommodate 35 ; adults, $8 to $10 ; special terms with more than one in room ; children over 4 and under 12, half price ; prefer not to take servants or very young children ; no transients, except friends of guests ; weekly rates. Raise all vegetables. Plenty eggs, milk, poultry, etc.

Joseph L. Reynolds—¼ mile. Accommodate 16 ; 9 rooms ; adults, $8 to $10; no small children ; no servants ; $1.50 per day. Raise and buy vegetables. Expect to furnish fresh eggs, milk and poultry.

L. E. Reynolds—3 miles. Conveyance, $1. Accommodation for 25 ; adults, $7 to $8. Small discount for season. Raises vegetables. Plenty of milk, eggs and poultry.

P M. Avery—¾ mile. Conveyance, 50 cents. Accommodations for 8 ; 4 rooms ; adults, $7 ; children, $3.50 ; servants, $5. Discount for season. Raises vegetables. Plenty of eggs, milk, poultry, etc.

Stephen A. Reynolds—¼ mile. Conveyance on arrival free. Accommodate 30 ; 15 rooms ; adults, $8 to $10 ; no servants ; $1.50 per day. Raise and buy vegetables. Milk, eggs and poultry.

Mrs. S. H. Royce—½ mile. Omnibus 10 cents. Accommodate 12 ; 7 rooms ; adults, $8 to $10 ; children and servants, $7 ; $1.50 per day. Fine location ; near church, public park and post office. Raise vegetables. Abundance of fresh milk, eggs and poultry.

FARM BOARDING HOUSES.

John Hill—3½ miles. Stage. Season guests, free conveyance. Accommodations for 20 ; 10 rooms, large ; adults, $6 and $7 ; children, $3. Plenty of shade. Large grounds. Fresh vegetables, milk butter, eggs, from farm. Furnish guides and livery.

Martin Toohey—Near Barnum's station, Port Jervis and Monticello R. R., 4 miles from Monticello. P. O. address, Monticello. Accommodations for 20 ; 10 rooms ; adults, $5 to $6 ; children, half price ; reduction for servants ; $1 per day, or 35 cents a meal ; Discount for season. House large and airy ; high ground. Fishing pond on farm. Three trains to Monticello daily ; fare, 15 cents each way. Pickerel and trout fishing near. Mail daily. Vegetables, etc., fresh from farm.

George Mapledoram—Near depot. Accommodations for 10 ; 2 must room together ; $5 the lowest rate. Romantic and sightly location. Shaded walks and retreats. Application must be made by June 1.

George W. Decker—2½ miles. Free conveyance. Accommodate 20 ; adults, 7 ; children and servants, by agreement. Best city references. Produce from farm. Horses furnished.

George McLoughlin—1 mile from depot. Conveyance free. Accommodations for 12 ; 6 rooms ; adults, $6 ; children, $3 ; servants, $5 ; $1 per day. Discount for large family for season. Large house ; pleasant rooms. Shady ground. Plenty of fresh eggs, milk, poultry and vegetables.

D. B. Bailey—3 miles. Conveyance free on arrival ; 50 cents returning. Accommodate 20 ; 12 rooms ; adults, $6 ; children $3 and $4 ; servants $4 and $5 ; $1.25 per day. Discount for season. High ground, surrounded by orchard trees. Two lakes within ½ mile. Bathing houses for ladies in Pleasant lake. Boats. Frequent straw rides free to guests. Fresh farm produce of all kinds.

William Carlisle—P. O. address, Mongaup Valley, Sullivan County, N. Y. 4 miles from Monticello. Stage, 25 cents ; will meet guests if desired. Accommodate 10 ; 6 rooms ; adults, $6 ; children, half price ; servants, $5 ; $1.25 per day. Discount for season. Raise all vegetables and provide eggs, milk and poultry from farm.

H. B. Reynolds—3 miles. Conveyance, 50 cents. Accommodation for 30 ; adults, $7 to $9. Small discount for season. Raises and buys vegetables. Plenty of milk, eggs, poultry, etc.

PRIVATE RESIDENCE.

Charles Ennis—P. O. Box 122, Monticello. Accommodate 8 persons ; adults preferred ; $6 to $8. Good table. For particulars, address as above.

Mrs. Agnes R. Crandall—¼ mile. 3 rooms ; adults, $8 ; children and servants, $5 ; $1.25 per day. Discount for season. Raises and buys vegetables. Plenty of eggs, milk, poultry, etc.

WHITE LAKE, SULLIVAN COUNTY, N. Y.

8 miles from Monticello ; stages connect with every train at that place. Fare to Lake, $1.

Largest of the many lakes of Sullivan County ; 1,500 feet above tide ; mountain scenery ; stocked with game fish. The black bass are marvels of size and flavor. Air similar to that in Hudson Highlands. Has been a popular resort for 40 years. No guides necessary.

BOARDING HOUSES.

"LAKE SHORE COTTAGE"—*John H. Corby, Proprietor*—Accommodate 35 ; 21 rooms ; adults, $8 ; children, $5 ; none under 7 years ; servants, $5 ; $1.50 per day. Discount for season. Western shore of lake. Free boats. Plenty of fresh vegetables, eggs, milk and poultry.

"VAN WERT HOUSE"—*W. A. Van Wert, Proprietor*—Accommodate 70 ; 40 rooms ; adults, $10 ; children, $3 to $7 ; servants, $6 ; $2 per day. Discount for season. Boats let, 50 cents a day. Raise and buy vegetables.

"MANSION HOUSE"—*D. B. Kinne, Proprietor*—Accommodate 100 ; 65 rooms ; adults, $7 to $10 ; servants, 5 ; $2 per day. Boats to let. Raise and buy vegetables.

"WHITE LAKE HOUSE"—*S. B. Kirk, Proprietor*—Accommodate 40 ; 16 rooms ; adults, $8 to $10 ; children and servants by contract ; $2 per day. Free boats. Vegetables raised on the farm. Fresh eggs, milk and poultry.

"SUNNY GLADE HOUSE"—*Mrs. M. A. B. Waddell, Proprietor*—Accommodate 20 ; adults, $8 to $10 ; children under 10, half price ; $1.50 per day. Boats free and to let. Raises vegetables. Abundance of milk, eggs and poultry.

"LAKE SIDE HOUSE"—*W. B. Gillespie. Proprietor*—Accommodate 40 ; 20 rooms ; adults, $8 to $10 ; children and servants, half price ; $2 per day. Discount for season. Fresh milk, eggs and poultry.

W. L. Merritt—Accommodate 40 ; 26 rooms : adults, $8 to $10 ; reduction for children and servants ; $2 per day. Discount for season. Raises vegetables. Plenty of fresh milk, eggs and poultry.

Thos. Steen—Accommodate 16 ; 8 rooms ; adults, $6.50 ; children under 12, half price ; servants, $5 ; $1.50 per day. Discount for season. Free boats and tackle. Raises vegetables. Plenty fresh milk, eggs and poultry.

ELLENVILLE, ULSTER COUNTY, N. Y.

90 miles from New York, via Erie Railway to Middletown, thence via Midland Railroad. FARE—LOCAL, $2.74 ; EXCURSION, $4.13.

This entire region is among the highest peaks of the Shawangunks, and in the heart of the Ulster and Sullivan trout and pickerel fishing. Ellenville is a charming village. Sam's point, 6 miles ; Lake Minnewaski, 7 miles ; the Ice Caves, 1 to 3 miles ; Honk Falls, 2 miles, are notable resorts and curiosities.   Good livery.

BOARDING HOUSES.

"TERRACE HILL"— *J. A. Meyers, Proprietor*—¾ mile.   Meets guests at depot.   Accommodations for 40 ; adults, $6 to $9 ; children, $3 to $6 ; $1.50 per day.   Rooms large, well furnished.   High ground.   Raises all vegetables.   Plenty fresh eggs. milk, poultry, etc.

J. F. Rhinehart —*P. O. address :   Napanoch, Ulster Co., N. Y.*— 2 miles.   Free conveyance.   Accommodate 14 : adults, $7 ; children and servants, half price ; $1 per day.   A trouting and gunning center.   Guides, $1 per day : furnishing tackle, dogs and guns.   Raises poultry, fruit and vegetables.   Plenty of milk and eggs fresh daily.   Livery attached ; $3 to $5 per day.

FARM HOUSE.

HILLSDALE HOUSE—*Edgar Vernooy, Proprietor*—P. O. address : Wawarsing, Ulster Co., N. Y.   7 miles from Ellenville.   Accommodations for 20 ; adults, $7.   Discount for season.   Best trout stream in the county near house ; partridge and other small game.   House 993 feet above tide.   Splendid grove.   Bold mountain scenery.

FALLSBURGH, SULLIVAN COUNTY, N. Y.

6 miles from Ellenville Junction of Midland.
FARE—LOCAL, $2.95 : EXCURSION, $4.55.

MUTTON HILL FARM HOUSE— *O. W. Bloxham, Proprietor*—P. O. address : Neversink, Sullivan County, N. Y.   10 miles.   Free conveyance. Beautiful drives.   Accommodate 30 ; 13 rooms : adults, $6 ; children under 10, $3 ; servants, $4 to 5 ; $1 per day.   Discount for season.   Trouting in Neversink and other streams : pickerel and perch in North, Gand, and Sheldrake lakes.   Partridge and other small game ; dog and gun.   High ground ; farm attached.   Guides procured.

LAKES MOHONK AND MINNEWASKA.

Via Erie Railway to Goshen ; thence via Montgomery Branch and Wallkill Valley Branch to New Paaltz ; thence via stage or carriage.

Among the highest and ruggedest peaks of the Shawangunk mountains, in Ulster County, N. Y., where only a few years since the foot of man had seldom trod, are a number of most remarkable and charming lakes, among them being Mohonk and Minnewaska.   The latter is on the rocky crest of a Shawangunk peak, near "Sam's Point," the great height that commands a view of the greater part of the Eastern and Middle States.   They are reached by an enjoyable drive from New Paaltz station.   Mohonk is 6, Minnewaska 16 miles from New Paaltz.

HOTELS.

At Mohonk—MOHONK LAKE HOUSE—*A. K. Smiley, Proprietor*—P. O. address : Mohonk Lake, Ulster Co., N. Y.   Accommodate 300 ; 200 rooms ; adults, $12 to $25 ; servants, $8 to $10 ; $2 to $4 per day ; stage meets all trains, $1.25.   Boats.   Livery.   Telegraph office.

At Minnewaska—MINNEWASKA HEIGHTS HOUSE—*A. K. Smiley, Proprietor*—Accommodate 250 ; 160 rooms ; adults, $12 to $18 ; no discount for children ; servants, $10 ; $2.50 to $3.00 per day. Discount for season. Mail daily.   P. O. address : Minnewaska, Ulster Co., N. Y.

AMONG THE DELAWARE HIGHLANDS.

SHOHOLA, PIKE COUNTY, PA.

107 miles from New York.   1 train from and 2 to New York daily ; train to New York Sundays.
FARE, $3.30 ; EXCURSION, $4.70.

On the banks of the Delaware, 1,000 feet above the sea.   Romantic Pike and Sullivan county scenery.   Shohola Glen, one mile from the station ; gorges, waterfalls, precipices, and deep pools.   Shohola creek, a celebrated trout stream, enters the Delaware here.   Panther brook, another trout stream, with fine cataracts, enters just above.   Falls of the Shohola great attraction.   Nine mountain lakes reached easily, farthest 6 miles. Hagan, Hagai, Big, Montgomery, Sand and York, in Sullivan County, and Big and Little Brink and Big and Little Walker, in Pike County, all stocked with bass and pickerel.   Bass fishing in the Delaware.   Dear, bear, fox, rabbit, partridge, and woodcock shooting.

Shohola is the station from which a picturesque portion of Sullivan County is reached, in the vicinity of Eldred among the Sullivan Highlands and lakes, 1,800 feet above tide.   A drive of five miles from Shohola.   One of the finest game and fishing regions in Sullivan County.

•   Guides to the hunting and fishing regions are numerous, both at Shohola and Eldred.   Their services command from $2 to $3 per day.

HOTEL.

SHOHOLA HOUSE- *Geo. Layman, Proprietor*—Near depot.   Accommodate 25 ; 14 rooms : adults, $6 to $8 : children, $3 to $4 ; servants, $5 ; $2 per day.   Discount for season.   Overlooks river.   Near glen.   Broad piazzas.   Furnishes livery.   Raises vegetables.   Plenty of fresh eggs, milk, and poultry.   Guides obtained.

BOARDING HOUSES.

Isaac M. Bradley—P. O. Address : Eldred, Sullivan Co., N. Y.—6 miles. Carriage, single passenger, $2 : family, $3 : Accommodate 15 ; 12 rooms ; adults, 1 in a room, $10 : 2 in a room, $7 each ; children and servants, $5 ; $1.25 and $1.50 per day.   Center of trout, perch, and pickerel fishing. Boats free.   Deer, bear, partridge, rabbit, woodcock, wild pigeon shooting. Deer-hounds and setters furnished : $2 per day.   Croquet ground.   Meet parties at Shohola when notified.   Headquarters for sportsmen.   Fresh vegetables, milk, eggs, and butter.   Guides obtained.

Myers, Mills & Co., Eldred, Sullivan Co., N. Y.—7 miles. Conveyance, 75 cents for one ; 50 cents for two or more ; trunks, 25 cents. Accommodate 30 ; 5 single rooms ; 12 double ; $6 to $8 ; $12 to $16 ; $1.25 per day. Discount for season. Lake in front of house ; 5 others within one mile. 2 boats free ; others 25 cents a day.

LITTLE POND COTTAGE—*J. Bodin, Proprietor—P. O. address : Eldred, Sullivan Co., N. Y.*—4 miles from depot. Accommodate 20 : 10 rooms, double piazzas all around ; adults, $8 to $10 ; $1.50 per day. Discount for season. Pond in front of house : 2 other ponds near. Conveyance, $1 per person from depot. French cooking. Fresh vegetables, milk, eggs, etc. Stabling for 3 horses. 1 boat free ; others 50 cents per day.

LACKAWAXEN, PIKE CO., PA.

111 miles from New York. 3 trains from and 3 trains to New York daily : 1 train from and 2 trains to New York Sunday.

FARE—LOCAL, $3.40 ; EXCURSION, $5.

Change cars for Millville (Blooming Grove Park), Hawley, and Honesdale.

— — —

On Delaware and Lackawaxen rivers, in hunting and fishing region of Pike and Wayne counties, Pa., and Sullivan county, N. Y. Surrounded by mountains and forests, streams and lakes. York lake, on summit of Sullivan County Highlands, 1,500 feet above tide, one mile distant. Wescoline lake four miles. The Delaware is formed into a broad lake by the Delaware and Hudson Canal Company's dam at Lackawaxen. Unexcelled boating and bass-fishing. Waterfalls on New York side of river. Trout streams—Lord's brook, one mile ; Panther brook, two miles ; Taylor's brook, five miles ; Shohola creek, six miles ; Beaver brook, three miles ; Blooming Grove and its streams, lakes, and hunting grounds, twelve miles, over a good road. Deer, bear, partridge, woodcock ; bass, trout, pickerel, eels, cat-fish. No mosquitoes or malaria.

HOTELS.

DELAWARE HOUSE—*F. J. Holbert, Manager*—⅓ of a mile. On banks of Delaware, at junction of Lackawaxen. Conveyance free. Accommodate 80; 55 rooms ; adults, May and June, $5 and $7 ; July and August, $8 and $12 ; September and October, $5 and $7. Children, $3 and $5 ; servants, $5 ; $2.50 per day during July and August. Two cottages near. Boating for a mile on river. Black bass fishing in front of house. Boats, 50 cents a day. Best of references. Fresh vegetables, butter, eggs, milk, etc., from farm. Guides obtained.

NATIONAL HOTEL—(Temperance)—*C. Van Benschoten, Proprietor*— Near depot. Highest ground in the place. Accommodations for 10 ; 15 rooms ; adults, $7 to $10 ; children, per agreement ; $2 per day. Discount for season. Furnishes livery. Boats free to guests. Vegetables raised on place and in vicinity. Keep cows and chickens. Guides obtained.

NARROWSBURG, SULLIVAN COUNTY, N. Y.

122¼ miles from New York. 3 trains from New York, 4 trains to New York daily ; 1 train from New York and 3 to New York Sunday.

FARE, $3.75 ; EXCURSION, $5.70.

On Delaware river at Big Eddy, widest and deepest part of Delaware river above tide ; literally a large lake of pure spring water. Black bass fishing. Boating for two miles. Ten mountain lakes within eight miles. Numerous trout streams in vicinity. No mosquitoes or malaria. Cool nights Deer hunting on surrounding ridges. Partridge shooting good. Splendid drives. A leading dining station of the Erie railway. Local sportsmen always ready to accompany visitors. Livery near station; $4 per day.

BOARDING HOUSE.

C. H. & C. J. Murray—Near depot. Accommodate 40; 20 rooms ; adults, $8 ; children under 10, half price ; servants, $7 ; $2 per day, Rooms large and airy. Broad piazza ; Everything first class. Good references. Also proprietors of dining hall in depot.

GEBHARD'S HOTEL—*J. Gebhard, Proprietor*—Near depot. Accommodate 15 ; 11 rooms ; adults, $7 ; children under 10, $4 ; servants, $5. Discount for season. Livery attached. Raises vegetables, eggs, milk, butter, poultry.

Mrs. G. Ughling's Hotel – (German) –Near depot. Accommodate 15; $6; $1 per day.

PRIVATE COTTAGE.

John D. Ruff—Near depot. Accommodate 10 ; 4 rooms ; adults, $7 to $8 ; children, half price ; servants, $5 ; $1.50 per day. Discount for season. Beautifully located on banks of the river at Big Eddy. 30 acres of lawn. Forest and fruit trees. Purest water. Fresh milk, eggs and vegetables.

FARM BOARDING HOUSE.

John Engleman—¼ mile. Free transportation. Near river. Accommodate 20 ; 12 rooms ; adults, $1 per day. Large, quiet farm house. Guides, dogs, no extra charge. Fresh eggs, milk, poultry and vegetables.

COCHECTON, SULLIVAN COUNTY, N. Y.

130¼ miles from New York. 1 train from, 2 trains to, New York daily ; 1 train to New York Sunday.

FARE, $4 ; EXCURSION, $6.20.

Quiet village on Delaware. Settled in 1752. Romantic location. Village of Damascus, Wayne County, Pa., opposite. Very healthful. No malaria or mosquitoes. Swago lake, 2 miles. Lake Huntington, 4 miles. Doughty pond and Cline pond, near. Best bass and pickerel fishing. Trout also in Lake Huntington. Bass in Delaware. Calkins, Page's, and Beaver Dam creeks, near. Trouting. Wild duck, partridge, deer. Livery and guides.

BOARDING HOUSE.

Leroy Bonesteel—¼ mile. P. O. address, Damascus, Wayne County, Pa. Free transportation. Accommodate 10 ; 6 rooms ; adults, $6 to $7 ; children, $3 to $5. Near Swago, Cline, Baird's and Laurel lakes. Bass and pickerel fishing and trout stream. Boat on Delaware river free. Raises vegetables, and obtains them in vicinity. Abundance of fresh milk, eggs, poultry and butter.

FARM HOUSES.

Ulysses Tyler—2½ miles. P. O. address, Damascus, Wayne County, Pa. Conveyance, 50 cents, after first trip. Accommodate 8 ; adults, $6 ; children, $4 ; servants, 5 ; $1 per day. Rooms high, light and airy. High ground. 1½ miles to Delaware river ; ¾ mile to Swago lake. Plenty shade. Plenty fresh milk, eggs, poultry and vegetables.

Miss Anna Doughty--4 miles. P. O. address, Damascus, Wayne County, Pa. For a party, conveyance, $1.50. Accommodate 20 ; 14 rooms : $6 for season guests ; servants, $6 ; $1 per day. Laurel lake on the place. Black bass, pickerel, perch, trout, near. Free boat. Guides secured. Conveyance furnished. Desire no children.

J. C. Perry—2 miles. P. O. address, Damascus, Wayne County, Pa. Conveyance free. Accommodate 10 ; 7 rooms ; adults, $5 to $8 ; children, $3 to $5 ; servants, $4. Discount for season. In the vicinity of best trout, bass, and pickerel fishing. Farm produce always fresh and abundant. Guides furnished.

CALLICOON, SULLIVAN COUNTY. N. Y.

136 miles from New York. 3 trains from and 2 trains to New York daily ; 1 train from New York Sunday.

FARE, $4.15 ; EXCURSION, $6.50.

Callicoon is the centre of one of the famous trout regions of the Delaware Valley. Callicoon creek, which enters the Delaware a short distance below station, threads the back wilderness and splendid farming section of Callicoon Valley. Along its entire course from the hills on either side, tributary streams flow into it at short intervals. The main stream and its feeders are natural trout creeks. These brooks are within an area of five miles. On Pennsylvania side of Delaware is Hollister creek. For two miles from the river this creek flows through a wild and narrow gorge, and seeks the level of the river by a series of waterfalls. Numerous lakes on both sides of river, as a glance at the map in this book will show. All the hotels and boarding houses give information as to guides.

HOTELS.

MINARD HOUSE.— *Z. Minard, Proprietor.* P. O. address, Callicoon Depot, Sullivan County, N. Y. Near depot. Accommodate 30 ; 30 rooms ; adults, $7 ; children, $3.50 ; servants, $5 ; $1.60 per day. Discount for season. Provides boats, guns and dogs, $1.50 per day. Livery, $2 per day for single rigs ; $3.50 per team. Plenty of fresh vegetables from hotel gardens.

WESTERN HOTEL.—*Mrs. L. Thorwelle, Proprietress.* P. O. address,

Callicoon Depot. Near depot. Accommodation for 40 ; 20 rooms ; adults, $6 to $8 single ; children, $3 to $4 ; servants, $4 ; $1.50 and $2 per day. Discount to season guests. Raises vegetables.

FALLS MILL HOUSE—*E. R. Lawrence, Proprietor*—P. O. address : Falls Mill, Sullivan Co., N. Y. 5 miles from depot. Will meet guests at train, free one way. Accommodations for 25 ; 15 rooms ; adults, $5 and $7 ; servants, $3 and $4 ; $1.50 per day. Discount for season. On the east branch of Callicoon creek. Best trout fishing and hunting. Large farm attached. Boats free.

CALLICOON HOTEL.—*John Ludwig, Proprietor*—P. O. address : Callicoon, Sullivan Co., N. Y. 9 miles from depot. Private conveyance and Stage, 50 cents. Accommodate 20 ; 20 rooms ; adults, $6 ; children, half price ; servants, $5 ; $1 per day. Discount for season. Near Post-office. Mail from New York at 5 P. M. Large farm attached. Streams so near no guide needed. Furnishes livery.

TRAVELER'S HOME—*C. Baurenfeind, Proprietor*—P. O. address : North Branch, Sullivan Co., N. Y. 5 miles. Free transportation. Accommodate 45 ; 18 rooms ; adults, $6 ; children, half price ; servants, $6. Raises vegetables.

PIKE POND HOTEL—*A. Grouten, Proprietor*—P. O. address : Pike Pond, Sullivan Co., N. Y. 8 miles. Stage. Accommodate 10 ; 10 rooms ; adults, $7 ; servants, $6 ; $1.25 per day. On the shore of Pike pond. Bass and pickerel. Free boats. Guns.

Geo. Filhoeber—P. O. address : North Branch, Sullivan County, N. Y. 5 miles. Conveyance free. Accommodate 20 ; 9 rooms ; adults, $6 ; children, $3 ; servants, $6. Raises vegetables. Abundance eggs, milk, poultry, etc.

BOARDING HOUSES.

HOTEL BRANDT—*A. Brandt, Proprietor*—P. O. address : Callicoon Depot N. Y. 2½ miles. Free conveyance. Accommodate 45 ; 20 rooms ; adults, $7 ; children, $3.50 ; $1.50 per day. Discount for season. Farm attached. Guides, dogs, guns, etc., furnished.

John Beck—P. O. address : Jeffersonville, Sullivan Co., N. Y. 10 miles. Stage or carriage. Accommodate 25 ; 10 rooms ; adults, $7 ; children, $4 to $6 ; servants, $5 to 6. Discount for season. Raises vegetables.

FARM HOUSES.

J. S. Gebhart—P. O. address : North Branch, Sullivan Co., N. Y. 5 miles. Platform spring wagon. Accommodate 12 ; 6 rooms ; $6 for adults. Raises vegetables. Fresh farm produce of all kinds.

Jacob Dietz—P. O. address : Callicoon, Sullivan Co., N. Y. 9 miles. Stage. Accommodate 12 ; $7 ; $1 per day.

Jno. Wolff—9 miles. P. O. address : Roscoe, Sullivan County, N. Y. Conveyance, 50 cents. Accommodate 50 ; 30 rooms ; adults, $6 ; children, half price ; servants, $4 ; $1 per day. Discount for season. Farm produce of all kinds in abundance. Fine, romantic location.

PRIVATE HOUSE.

E. Fish—P. O. address : Jeffersonville, Sullivan Co., N. Y. 9 miles. Carriage free one way. Accommodate 25 ; adults, $6 and upward ; discount for season. Would like school of children of 25 or 30 for season. Reasonable terms. Plenty shade. Dry surroundings. Daily mail. Fresh milk, eggs, butter, poultry and vegetables.

STAGE LINES.

For North Branch (50 cents) and Callicoon (75 cents), Tuesdays, Thursdays, and Saturdays. For Jeffersonville and Pike Pond, daily except Sunday, $1 ; $1.50 round trip. Leave after the arrival train 1 (9.15 A. M. from New York). Connect with train 30 for New York (2.52 P. M.)

HANKINS, DELAWARE COUNTY, N. Y.

144½ miles from New York. 1 train from and 1 train to New York daily except Sunday.
FARE, $4.35.

A station among the upper Delaware mountains. Splendid country back on the hills. Fine scenery. Best of trout and bass fishing. Deer, partridge and small game in season. Long pond, Basket pond, Mott pond, Low pond, Hankins creek, Basket Creek, Back brook, Centre creek, Trout creek, and others, in the vicinity.

BOARDING HOUSES.

Philemon Minkler—4 miles. P. O. address : Fremont Centre, Sullivan Co., N. Y. Conveyance, $2 per trip. Accommodations for 30 ; 15 rooms ; adults, $6 ; children, $3 to $4 ; servants, $4 ; $1 per day. Discount for season. Near village, with post-office, stores, hotels, churches, schools, etc. Good place for children. Swings and other amusements. Good spring water. Farm house, enlarged expressly for summer guests. Boats free. Will act as guide, $2 per day. Raises vegetables. Specialty of fresh milk, eggs and poultry. Livery convenient.

Jno. W. Kessler—2½ miles. Free conveyance. Accommodation for 15 ; 6 large rooms ; adults, $6 ; children, $3 ; servants, $4 ; $1 per day. Families preferred. On main road to Hankins depot ; on Hankins Creek. Trouting. Livery. Raise and buy vegetables. Plenty of fresh milk, eggs and poultry.

Andrew Boyer—4½ miles. Conveyance, $1. Accommodate 80 ; adults, $6 ; children, $3.50 ; 40 cents a meal. Discount for season. Raises vegetables. Plenty of all desirable farm produce. Livery.

HANCOCK, DELAWARE COUNTY. N. Y.

164 Miles from New York. 4 trains each way daily ; 1 train from and 3 trains to New York Sunday:
FARE, $5.

At the junction of the two branches of the Delaware river. Surrounded by mountains. Fifteen trout streams within from one to twelve miles. In the Beaverkill region. Ten lakes near. Deer, bear, partridge. Black bass in the Delaware. Good livery.

HOTEL.

HANCOCK HOUSE—*E. W. Griffis, Proprietor*—Near depot. Accommodations for 25 ; 40 rooms : $6 ; $1.60 per day. Discount for season.

In the Hudson Highlands.

ALONG THE NEWBURGH SHORT CUT.

Aside from the delightful scenery of the Highlands, it is a fact which the experience of years has demonstrated that the air which circulates among these hills and valleys is possessed of curative properties that render the existence of pulmonary or bronchial difficulties next to an impossibility from the Schunemunk range to the Cornwall hills. It is stated that there is a well defined line which marks the boundary of this rare mountain atmosphere, and that the area of its presence is within the mountain elevations just mentioned. There are innumerable instances of invalids being restored to robust health by a few seasons spent in the Highlands, prominent among them being the late N. P. Willis, the poet, who visited Cornwall a confirmed consumptive, spent one season among the mountains, and was so much benefited that he became a resident, and was restored to health. The value of this region as a sanitarium is now recognized by leading physicians, and many patients suffering with lung or throat diseases are annually recommended by them to seek some one of the favorite resorts among the Highlands, on the line of the Erie Railway.

CENTRAL VALLEY, ORANGE COUNTY, N. Y.

48¾ miles from New York. 5 trains from and 6 to New York daily; 1 from and 2 to New York Sunday.

SUMMER FARE—LOCAL, $1.15; EXCURSION, $2. COMMUTATION, 3 MONTHS, $42.75.

HOTEL.

SUMMIT LAKE HOUSE—*Elisha Stockbridge, Proprietor*—2 miles. Carriage and stage, 50 cents. Accommodations for 125; 52 rooms; adults, $8 to $15; children, $7; servants, $7; $2 per day. Discount to season guests. In heart of the Highlands. 1,800 feet above tide. 11 mountain lakes. Summit lake near. Bass and pickerel. Boats and tackle furnished guests; 10 cents per hour, 50 cents per day; boat extra. Woodcock, partridge, fox, rabbit. Sam Weeks acts as guide to lakes and hunting ground; $1 per day. Vegetables, fruits, eggs, milk, chickens, butter, all from the place. Livery attached.

BOARDING HOUSES.

LOCUST LAWN HOUSE—*Isaac L. Noxen, Proprietor*—½ mile. Conveyance free on arrival of guest and departure at end of season. Accommodate

40 to 50 ; 26 rooms ; adults, $7 to $10 ; children, $2 to $5 ; servants, $5 to $7 ; $1.50 per day. Discount to season guests. Special rates to families. Vegetables, fruit, milk, eggs, chickens and butter all from the place. Pickerel and bass lakes within easy reach.

David Cornell —¼ mile from depot. Accommodations for 25 ; 17 rooms ; adults, $7 ; children, $5 ; servants, $5 ; $1 per day. Discount for large families. Near lakes. Vegetables, milk, eggs, butter from the place.

F. F. Oram —½ mile. Conveyance free. Accommodations for 40 ; 22 rooms ; adults, $8 ; children, $4 ; servants, $5. Raise vegetables. Plenty of fresh eggs, milk and poultry.

FARM HOUSE.

MAPLE FARM—*Mrs. H. Thorne, Sr.*—Near. Accommodations for 10 ; 7 rooms ; adults, 8 ; children, $4 ; servants, $6. Fresh milk, eggs, poultry and vegetables.

HIGHLAND MILLS, ORANGE COUNTY, N. Y.

49½ miles from New York. 5 trains from and 6 to New York daily ; 1 train from and 2 to New York Sunday.

SUMMER FARES—LOCAL, $1.15 ; EXCURSION, $2. COMMUTATION, 3 MONTHS, $43.25.

HOTELS.

CROMWELL LAKE HOUSE—*Oliver Cromwell, Proprietor*—1½ miles. Stage meets all trains : 25 cents. Accommodates 125 ; 70 rooms : adults, $8 to $10 ; children, $5 to $8 ; servants, $5 to $8 ; $2.00 per day. Discount for season. Vegetables raised in vicinity. Plenty of fresh eggs, milk and poultry.

WOODBURY, ORANGE COUNTY. N. Y.

50¾ miles from New York. 5 trains from and 6 to New York daily ; 1 train from and 2 to New York Sunday.

SUMMER FARES—LOCAL, $1.15 ; EXCURSION, $2. COMMUTATION, 3 MONTHS, $43.75.

BOARDING HOUSES.

MAPLE CENTRE FARM—*Lewis S. Joyce, Proprietor*—¼ mile. Carriage, 15 cents. Accommodations for 25 ; 13 rooms ; adults, $7 to $8 ; children $4 to $5; servants, $6 ; $1.50 per day. A creek runs through the premises. Within easy reach of all the lakes. Furnishes livery. Raises vegetables. Furnishes milk, eggs and poultry fresh daily. P. O. address, Woodbury Falls, Orange County, N. Y.

L. A. Van Cleft—⅛ mile. Free conveyance. Accommodate 30 ; 14 rooms ; adults, $8 to $10 : children and servants, $5 to $7 ; $2 per day. Discount for season. Raises vegetables. Furnishes livery. Guides. Cottages near. P. O. address, Woodbury Falls, Orange County, N. Y.

MOUNTAINVILLE, ORANGE COUNTY, N. Y.

54½ miles from New York. 5 trains from, 6 trams to New York daily; Sunday, 1 train from, 2 trains to New York.

SUMMER FARES—LOCAL, $1.15 ; EXCURSION, $2. COMMUTATION, 3 MONTHS, $46.

BOARDING HOUSES.

John Orr—Near depot. Accommodations for 40 : 14 rooms ; adults, $10 ; children, $4 to $6 ; servants, $5 ; $1.50 per day. Cottage, 5 rooms, near. Spring water. Furnishes livery. Raises vegetables. Fresh milk, eggs, and poultry.

N. D. Brown—1½ mile. Conveyance 50 cents. Accommodate 18 ; 6 large rooms ; adults, $8 ; children, $4 and $5 ; servants, $5 ; $1.50 per day. Raises vegetables. Plenty of fresh milk, eggs and poultry.

A. Freudenburgh—½ mile. Accommodations for 60 ; adults, $6 and upwards ; children under 12 half price ; servants half price ; $1.25 per day. Plenty of fruit. Well water so cold that no ice is necessary. Cornwall Mineral Spring one-half mile. Extra stalls for boarding horses. Farm boarding-house.

FARM HOUSE.

Jacob Smith—¾ mile. Accommodations for 20 ; 7 rooms ; adults, $7 ; children, $4 ; servants, $5. Raises vegetables. Plenty of eggs, milk and poultry.

CORNWALL, ORANGE COUNTY, N. Y.

56 miles from New York. 5 trains from New York and 6 to New York daily ; 1 train from and 2 to New York Sunday.

SUMMER FARES—LOCAL, $1.15 ; EXCURSION, $2 ; COMMUTATION, 3 MONTHS, $46.75 ; BOOK OF 50 TICKETS, $30, VALID 3 MONTHS, EITHER DIRECTION.

Not less than five thousand people annually summer in the Cornwall district, and among the guests who are now regular annual visitors there are many who came to Cornwall as invalids years ago. Physicians send patients to Cornwall for affections that it was formerly thought could not be benefited in a climate other than the Bahamas, Bermudas, or the Lake Superior region. Storm King and Old Cro' Nest, two ancient crags, belong to Cornwall. The drives to West Point, to Newburgh, to New Windsor, and the hundreds of shorter mountain drives and walks, are unsurpassed. Good livery in the place.

BOARDING HOUSES.

LINDEN PARK HOUSE—*R. B. King, Proprietor*—1½ mile from depot. Stage 25 cents. Accommodations for 80 ; 35 rooms : adults, $8 to $12 ; children under 5, $4, over that, full price : servants, $7 ; $2 per day. Discount to season guests. Everything first-class. Raises fruit and vegetables.

MOODNA MANSION—*Wm. Orr, Proprietor*—¼ mile. Stage 15 cents. Accommodate 60, with cottage ; 30 rooms ; 1 in room, $8 to $10 ; 2 in room, $6 to $8 ; servants, $5 per week ; $2 per day. Discount for season. Livery in connection with house. Raises vegetables. Plenty of milk, eggs, etc.

L. P. Clark—P. O. address : Cornwall-on-the-Hudson, N. Y.—2½ miles.
Accommodate 16 ; 9 rooms ; adults, $10 ; take no children or servants ; $2
per day. Boats and tackle. Raises vegetables. Plenty of milk, eggs and
poultry.

LAWRENCE HOUSE—*J. J. Lawrence, Proprietor*—3 miles. Stage 25
cents. Accommodations for 70 in large house, 12 in small house (adults
only) ; 28 rooms in large house, 6 in small ; adults, $8 to $12 ; servants, $6 ;
$2 per day. Discount for season. Raises fruit and vegetables.

VINEBROOK COTTAGE—*Mrs. C. E. Cocks, Proprietor*—2½ miles. Stage
25 cents. Accommodate 20 ; 10 rooms ; adults, $8 ; children, $4 to $7 ;
$1.50 per day. Discount to season guests. Five minutes from post-office,
telegraph office, and reading room. Farm of 11 acres. Adjoins farm of
E. P. Roe, the author and fruit cultivator. Base of Storm King. Plenty of
fresh fruit. Boats by day or week for rowing. Make a specialty of our
table. Everything fresh.

LEBANON HOUSE—*Josiah Clark, Proprietor—P. O. address : Cornwall-
on-the-Hudson*—2½ miles. Stage 25 cents. Accommodate 50 ; 20 rooms ;
adults, $7 to $10 ; children and servants half price ; $1.50 to $2 per day.
Plenty of fresh vegetables, milk, eggs, poultry, etc. Livery furnished.

NEWBURGH, ORANGE COUNTY, N. Y.

63½ miles from New York. 5 trains from New York and 6 trains to New York daily ;
1 train from and 2 trains to New York Sunday.

SUMMER FARES—LOCAL, $1.20 ; EXCURSION, $2.25. COMMUTATION, 3 MONTHS, $50 ; BOOK
OF 50 TICKETS, $32.50. VALID FOR 3 MONTHS, EITHER DIRECTION.

Population, 20,000. On Newburgh Bay. First settled in 1719. Celebrated for its Revolutionary associations, beautiful scenery, and healthfulness. Washington's Headquarters in 1782-3. Famous building occupied
by him, erected in 1752, still standing. Filled with relics of the Revolution.
Unsurpassed boating and fishing in the Bay. Orange lake, 6 miles distant ;
bass and pickerel. Fine drives to Cornwall, West Point, and all places in
Highlands. Churches of all denominations. Guides, $1.50 per day.

BOARDING HOUSES.

J. Baldwin—½ mile. Free 'bus. 25c. per trunk. Accommodation for
200 ; 83 rooms ; 1 in room, $10 to $20 ; 2 or more, $8 to $12 each ; children
and servants, ⅔ rate ; $2.50 and $3 per day. Discount for season. All
vegetables raised in vicinity. Plenty fresh milk, butter, eggs and poultry.
Livery, single rigs, $1 per hour ; double, with or without driver, $1.50 per
hour. Special rates for long distance, or all day.

H. W. Murtfelt—3 miles. Livery conveyance. Accommodate 35 ; 15
rooms ; adults, $8 to $10 ; children under 8, half price ; servants, $4 to $5.
On the banks of the Hudson. Fine drives and walks. Plenty of fruit,
vegetables, milk, eggs, poultry, etc. P. O. Box 199.

THE LACKAWAXEN VALLEY.

VIA HONESDALE BRANCH FROM LACKAWAXEN.

———— • ————

MILLVILLE, PIKE COUNTY, PA.

——

119 miles from New York. 1 train from New York daily, except Sunday; 2 on Wednesdays and Saturdays; 2 trains to New York daily, except Sunday.

FARE, $3.70. EXCURSION, $5.50.

Centre of a noted hunting and fishing region. Tink, Big and Little Corilla, Knob, White Deer, and Jones's lakes are within a radius of seven miles. Several beautiful waterfalls near. Station for Blooming Grove Park, the famous game preserve of 12,000 acres, and M. C. Westbrook's popular Blooming Grove retreat. Distance, 7 miles. Livery furnished at Millville, by John Deming, who also keeps a good hotel for the accommodation of visitors.

HOTELS.

WESTBROOK HOUSE.—*M. C. Westbrook, Proprietor* P. O. address, Blooming Grove, Pike County, Pa.—8 miles. Conveyance, $1. Accommodations for 25 ; 15 rooms ; adults, $7 to $10 ; children half price ; $1.50 per day. In the midst of the Blooming Grove hunting and fishing region. Grand mountain scenery. High Knob, loftiest elevation in Northern Pennsylvania, 2,000 feet above tide, 3 miles. Three lakes on the summit of this mountain. Black bass, trout and pickerel fishing unsurpassed. The greatest deer and bear region in the State. Partridge and woodcock. Guides furnished, $1 per day. Guns, dogs and fishing-tackle. Livery attached. Large farm and dairy.

BLOOMING GROVE PARK CLUB HOUSE—8 miles from depot. On shores of Lake Giles. Carriage. Accommodations for 100. Terms arranged on application. Deer, bear and all small game in the preserve. Eight large lakes, stocked with bass, pickerel and perch. A score of trout streams. A retreat for gentlemen sportsmen and their families.

HAWLEY, WAYNE COUNTY, PA.

——

127 miles from New York. Same train facilites as Millville.

FARE, $3.90 ; EXCURSION, $5.75.

In the Pike County game and fish region. Trout, bass and pickerel ; deer, bear, fox, partridge, rabbits. The wonderful Wallenpaupack Falls in

36

the village. Terminus of the famous Gravity Railroad of the Pennsylvania Coal Company. One of the grandest excursion routes in America. Scranton, 35 miles, heart of Lackawanna coal region. Lake Jones, 6 miles; White Deer lake, 9 miles; Trout streams, from 1 to 8 miles. Also station for Blooming Grove. Good hotels. But make no specialty of keeping summer boarders. Good livery.

HONESDALE, WAYNE COUNTY, PA.

136 miles from New York. Same train facilities as Millville.
FARE, $4.40 ; EXCURSION, $6.75.

One of the handsomest and wealthiest villages in Pennsylvania. Lackawaxen and Dyberry rivers run through the place. Streets broad and bordered with maples and elms fifty years old. Excellent drives. Bethany, 3 miles : Mart Kimble's, 2 miles ; White Mills, 5 miles ; Waymart, 10 miles. Beautiful park of maples in center of village. Twelve famous bass and pickerel lakes within from six to fourteen miles. Trout fishing within from two to five miles. Terminus of the celebrated Gravity Railroad owned by the Delaware and Hudson Canal Company. This road extends to Carbondale, 17 miles, in the upper Lackawanna coal regions. In connection with the similar road from Hawley, it is now one of the most popular excursion roads in America. The cars run up and down high hills, there being no motive power perceptible to the tourist. At one point, an elevation of 2,000 feet above tide is reached. The road curves abruptly around mountains, and traverses glens and the sides of lofty hills. The ride is exhilerating, grand, indescribable. Hundreds of tourists enjoy it daily during the summer and fall months. The Honesdale livery accommodations are excellent.

HOTELS.

ALLEN HOUSE—*M. B. Allen, Proprietor*—1 mile. Omnibus, 25 cents ; or will meet guests, if notified. Accommodations for 50 ; fine large and airy double and single rooms ; $6 to $10. Special arrangement with season guests. Overlooks park. Splendid location. Broad halls, balconies. Commodious stables. Bath. Vegetables from farm. Free transportation to and from Gravity depots.

KIMBLE HOUSE—*M. K. Kimble, Proprietor*—2 miles. Meets guests at depot with private conveyance. Accommodations for 14 ; 11 rooms ; $6 to $7 ; $1 per day. Beautiful location. Large farm attached. Surrounded by large shade trees. Dyberry river runs through the place. Boating and fishing. Croquet lawn. Commodious stables. All equipments for sportsmen. Plenty of fresh vegetables, fruit, eggs, butter and milk. Boats provided. Conveyance furnished on reasonable terms.

On The Newburgh Branch.

West of the Schunemunk mountains is the romantic valley of the Murderer's Kill, through which the branch of the Erie Railway extending from Greycourt to Newburgh passes. The valley, like this entire section of Orange County, is full of historical associations. The Newburgh Branch and the Short Cut unite at Vail's Gate, six miles from Newburgh. It was at the former place that Generals St. Clair and Gates were quartered when the army was encamped in the vicinity. The Edmoston House, their headquarters, is still standing. It was built in 1755. At Washington Square, two miles from Vail's Gate, General Clinton had his headquarters in the Falls House, still intact. An ancient Indian burying-ground, and a number of very old churches are in the vicinity. Pickerel, bass, and perch fishing in the adjacent lakes. Livery at all the stations.

CRAIGVILLE, ORANGE CO., N. Y.

56¼ miles from New York. 3 trains from and 4 to New York daily ; 1 train each way Sunday.

FARE—LOCAL, $1.70 ; EXCURSION, $2.30. COMMUTATION, 3 MONTHS, $47.45.

FARM HOUSE.

Dr. Wm. Horton—¾ mile. Conveyance free ; meet all guests. Accommodate 30 ; 14 rooms ; adults, $6 to $8 ; children, $3 to $5 ; $1.50 per day. Discount for season. Three cottages near Raise vegetables.

WASHINGTONVILLE, ORANGE COUNTY, N. Y.

61 Miles from New York. 3 trains from and 4 to New York daily ; 1 train each way Sunday.

FARE—LOCAL, $1.85 ; EXCURSION, $2.50. COMMUTATION, 3 MONTHS. $50.50.

BOARDING HOUSES.

Miss A. E. Brooks—Five minutes' walk from depot. Accommodate 14 ; adults, $6 to $8 ; reduction for children ; servants, $5 to $6 ; $1.50 per day. Discount for season. Raises vegetables. Abundance of fresh eggs, milk, poultry, etc.

T. B. Cameron—¼ mile from depot. Accommodations for 20 ; 4 single rooms ; 5 very large double rooms ; $6 single ; $8 double ; $1.50 per day. Has a horse and carriage. Vegetables and fruit raised on place and in vicinity.

FARM HOUSES.

Miss M. Beatty—3 miles. Conveyance free. Baggage, $1 each way. Accommodate 15 ; 6 large rooms ; adults, $6 to $8 ; young children, $3 ; servants, $5 and $6 ; $1.50 per day. Discount for season. Broad piazzas. Extensive grounds. Plenty of shade. Vegetables, fruits, eggs, butter and milk. Furnishes conveyance, stabling and carriage room.

SALISBURY, ORANGE COUNTY, N. Y.

63½ miles from New York. 3 trains from and 4 to New York daily ; 1 train each way Sunday.

FARE—LOCAL, $1.95 ; EXCURSION, $2.60. COMMUTATION, 3 MONTHS, $52.

WOANGDALE VILLA—*R. Wallace Genung, Proprietor*—2½ miles. Carriage free. Accommodate 14 ; 7 rooms ; adults, $8 to $10 ; children under 12 half price ; servants, $5 ; $1.50 per day. Discount for season. 450 feet above the Hudson at Newburg, 8 miles distant. Not one case of malaria in 50 years in the neighborhood. Near old Governor Clinton homestead. One mile from Highlands. Fresh vegetables, fruit, eggs, milk and butter. Livery at Salisbury station. P. O. address : Salisbury Mills, Orange Co., N. Y.

STONE BRIDGE, ORANGE COUNTY, N. Y.

62 miles from New York via Erie Railway to Greycourt, thence via Lehigh and Hudson River R. R.

FARE—LOCAL, $1.90.

Scenery unsurpassed in Orange County. Healthful, mountainous, and near lakes and streams.

BOARDING HOUSE.

Wm. H. Wisner—2 miles. P. O. address : Bellvale, Orange Co., N. Y. Free conveyance. Accommodate 20 ; 9 rooms ; adults, $7 ; children and servants, $5 ; $1.95 per day. Broad verandas. Shaded lawn. Pleasant walks and drives. Rooms large and airy. Raise vegetables. Plenty fresh milk, eggs, poultry, etc.

WARWICK, ORANGE COUNTY, N. Y.

64½ miles from New York, via Erie Railroad to Greycourt; thence via Lehigh and Hudson River R. R.

FARE—LOCAL, $1.95 ; EXCURSION, $2.75. COMMUTATION, 3 MONTHS, $56.25.

Warwick and region around it furnish great attraction to the tourist. Sugar-Loaf mountain, Sterling mountain, Mount Adam and Mount Eve, notable features of the landscape. Old Sterling iron-furnace, near outlet of Sterling lake. Founded by Lord Sterling in 1751. Partridge, quail, woodcock, pickerel, black bass. Greenwood lake, 6½ miles ; Glenmere, 4½ miles ; Wawayanda lake, 7½ miles ; Double lake, 5 miles ; Wickham's lake, 3 miles. Tackle provided at them all. Warwick Woodlands near. Good livery.

BOARDING HOUSES.

Mrs. William L. Benedict—½ mile. Conveyance, 25 cents. Accommodations for 30 : 14 rooms ; adults, $6 to $8 ; children, $2 to $4, according to age : servants, $4 to $5 : $1 per day. Spacious grounds, well shaded. Surroundings cheerful, healthful and attractive. Abundance of vegetables, fruit, milk, eggs and butter.

Mrs. J. C. Sly, Jr. & Mrs. H. A. Roy—2½ miles from Warwick. Conveyance free. Accommodate 10 ; 4 rooms, large ; adults, $7 ; children, $3 : servants, $5. Raise vegetables. Fresh eggs, poultry and milk.

FARM HOUSE.

KILCARE COTTAGE—*A. M. Hoyt, Proprietor*—3 miles. Free carriage. Accommodations for 25 ; adults, $7. Woods and mountains ; 9 miles from Greenwood lake ; 4 miles from Wawayanda lake. Fresh farm products daily.

Charles Gale—2½ miles. Conveyance for guests remaining one week or over. free ; less time, $1 to and from depot. Accommodations for 15 ; 6 rooms ; adults, $6 ; children under 10, $4 ; over 10, $5 ; servants, $5 ; $1 per day. Discount for season. A pleasant, agreeable house. Veal, mutton, lamb and poultry raised and killed on place. Well and spring water. Plenty of fresh eggs, milk and butter.

In the Catskills.

<hr>

VIA ERIE RAILWAY TO GOSHEN, THENCE VIA MONTGOMERY BRANCH AND WALLKILL VALLEY RAILROAD TO KINGSTON, THENCE VIA ULSTER AND DELAWARE RAILROAD.

SHOKAN, ULSTER COUNTY, N. Y.

18 miles from Kingston.

FARM BOARDING HOUSE.

J. M. Burgher—2 miles. Conveyance free for season guests. P. O. address, West Shokan, Ulster County, N. Y. Accommodate 25 ; 12 rooms ; adults, $6 to $8 ; children, $3 and $4 ; servants, $4 ; $1 per day. Near Whitenburg, Bushkill and Rondout creeks. Trout, woodcock, quail and partridge. Obtain guides. Farm produce fresh and abundant.

BIG INDIAN, ULSTER COUNTY, N. Y.

36 miles from Kingston.

BOARDING HOUSE.

SLIDE MOUNTAIN HOUSE—*B. Dutcher, Proprietor*—3 miles. Conveyance, 50 cents. Accommodate 40 ; adults, $5 to $7 ; children, half price ; servants, $5 ; $1.25 per day. Discount for season. Near base of Slide mountain. Trout fishing in head waters of Neversink and Beaverkill streams. Guides provided. Four trout ponds on place. Table supplied with trout daily. Plenty of fresh eggs, milk, poultry, etc. Open June 1.

WHEN SPORT IS LEGAL.

The following is a brief digest of the game-laws of the three States mentioned therein, as they relate to the regions in which the Erie Resorts are located. It is compiled from the laws of 1882, those for 1883 not being perfected and issued at the date of compilation. It is not likely, however, that the new laws will make any material changes in those of 1882, as affecting these regions.

FISHING.

BROOK TROUT.

New Jersey—March 1 to October 1. *New York*—April 1 to September 1. *Pennsylvania*—April 1 to August 1, *except in Pike County;* in that county from May 1 to August 1.

BLACK BASS.

New Jersey—July 1 to November 1. *New York*—June 1 to January 1. *Pennsylvania*—June 1 to January 1.

PICKEREL.

New Jersey—June 1 to January 1. *New York*—June 1 to January 1. *Pennsylvania*—June 1 to January 1, *except in Pike County;* in that county from June 1 to February 15.

HUNTING.

WOODCOCK.

New Jersey—July 1 to August 1; September 30 to December 16. *New York*—August 1 to January 1. *Pennsylvania*—July 4 to January 1, *except in Pike County;* in that county from July 4 to December 15.

RUFFED GROUSE (Partridge or Pheasant.)

New Jersey—November 1 to January 1. *New York*—September 1 to January 1. *Pennsylvania*—October 1 to January 1, *except in Pike County;* in that county from September 15 to December 15.

QUAIL.

New Jersey—November 1 to January 1. *New York*—November 1 to January 1. *Pennsylvania*—October 15 to January 1.

WILD DUCK.

New Jersey—September 1 to January 1. *New York*—May 1 to October 1. *Pennsylvania*—May 15 to October 1, *except in Pike County ;* in that county from October 1 to January 1.

DEER.

New Jersey—October 15 to January 1. *New York*—August 1 to December 1. *Pennsylvania*—October 1 to January 1, *except in Pike County ;* in that county from October 1 to December 1.

RABBIT or HARE.

New Jersey—November 1 to January 1. *New York*—November 1 to February 1. *Pennsylvania*—November 1 to January 1, *except in Pike County ;* in that county from October 15 to December 15.

SQUIRRELS.

New Jersey—September 1 to January 1. *New York*—August 1 to February 1. *Pennsylvania*—September 1 to January 1, *except in Pike County ;* in that county from September 1 to December 15.

NOTES.

In New York State robins and meadow larks may be killed during the months of October, November and December. In the other States they are protected by law the year round, except for scientific purposes.

Fishing or hunting on Sunday is illegal in Pennsylvania, and is punishable with a fine of $25 for each offense. It is also against the law in that State to have in possession a brook trout under *five inches* in length.

Taking the different fishes mentioned in the above digest by other means than hook or line, or snaring or trapping the game birds mentioned, or using punt guns or swivels, are illegal, and punishable with heavy fines.

In Pennsylvania it is illegal to run deer with dogs, or kill any deer in waters where it may have been driven. Dogs may be employed in New York State from August 15 to November 1. It is illegal in this State to kill a spotted fawn.

Wild pigeon may be killed at any time in the above States excepting during the nesting season.

IMPORTANT TO TRAVELERS.

Time Limit of Excursion Tickets.

For all stations on the Eastern Division and branches between and including Port Jervis and Suffern, Excursion Tickets will be valid on day of date and *two days* thereafter.

For Pond Eddy and Shohola, on the Delaware Division, Excursion Tickets will be valid on day of date and *three days* thereafter.

For Lackawaxen, Narrowsburg, Cochecton, and Callicoon, on the Delaware Division, and for stations on the Honesdale Branch, Excursion Tickets will be valid on day of date and *four days* thereafter.

☞ Excursion Tickets will be good for continuous passage on passenger trains stopping as per time table at the stations named on the tickets, during the time limit as stated on their face, but will not be honored after the expiration of the time limit. Except that in the case of Excursion Tickets to or from New York or Jersey City, on which the printed time limit is *five days or less*, if a Sunday or legal holiday intervenes between the date of purchase and the expiration of the time limit such tickets will be valid for as many additional days as there are Sundays or legal holidays included in the printed time limit.

Commutation tickets may be obtained at the Ticket Office, 187 West Street.

All information as to travel over the Erie Railway, tickets, rates, maps, time-tables, etc., may be obtained on application at the Ticket Offices of the Company, 261, 401, 957 Broadway, and 187 West Street, N. Y.; No. 2 Court Street, Brooklyn; 34 Hudson Street, Hoboken, N. J.; 184 Market Street, Newark; at the depots foot of Chambers Street, or 23d Street, North River, and in Jersey City.

All trains on the Erie Railway leave New York from the foot of Chambers Street, and 23d Street.

JNO. N. ABBOTT,

General Passenger Agent,

21 Courtlandt St., N. Y.

44

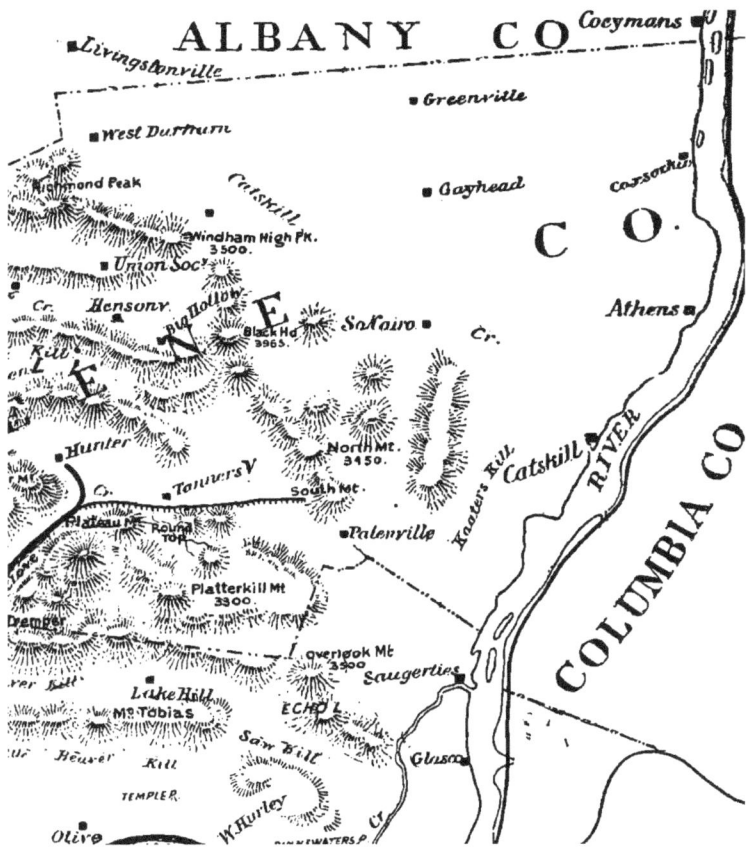

ALBANY CO. Coeymans

Livingstonville

Greenville

West Durham

Richmond Peak

Catskill

Gayhead

Corsochin

Windham High Pk.
3500.

C O.

Union Soc?

Henson.

Big Hollow

Black He.
3965.

So Kairo

Cr.

Athens

Kill

Hunter

Cr.

North Mt.
3450.

Tannersv

South Mt.

Kaaters Kill

Catskill

RIVER

Plateau Mt.

Round Top

Palenville

Platterkill Mt.
3300

Dremps

Overlook Mt.
3500

Saugerties

Lake Hill

Mt Tobias

ECHO L.

COLUMBIA CO

Saw Bill

Heaver

Kill

Glasco

TEMPLE R.

W. Hurley

Olive

RINKWATERS P.

Cr.

www.ingramcontent.com/pod-product-compliance
Lightning Source LLC
Chambersburg PA
CBHW021435090426
42739CB00009B/1489